Infinite Shades of Happiness
Love & Online Dating

I0089901

Part One: Millennials

André Prince de Grâce

Agora Books

Agora Books
Ottawa, Canada

Infinite Shades of Happiness
Love & Online Dating

c. 2019, by André Prince de Grâce

All Rights Reserved. No part of this book may be reproduced, stored in a retrieval system, or transmitted, in any form or by any means, electronic, mechanical, photocopying, recording or otherwise, without the expressed written consent of Agora Books.

The views, opinions and perceptions of the author of the book herein expressed in this text are intended to support civil and creative social discussion in Canada and internationally.

Care has been taken to trace the ownership/source of any references made in this text. The publisher welcomes any information that will enable a rectification in subsequent edition(s) of any incorrect or omitted reference or credit.

Agora Books
B.P. 24191
300 Eagleson Rd.
Kanata, Ontario K2M 2C3 CANADA

Agora Books is a trade mark of The Agora Cosmopolitan which is a not-for-profit corporation.

ISBN - 978-1-927538-38-8

Printed in Canada

Acknowledgements

First, I would like to thank my wonderful readers for daring to venture into the online dating world. Please, take a breath and gather the courage to join me in my incredible journey into the often misunderstood world of online dating which offers the ultimate goal of finding LOVE. Through my *online dating saga*, it is my goal to transcend the walls of misunderstanding which often plague the interactions between men and women as they attempt to interact online. May your reading journey with this story provide you laughter, joy and a relaxed experience!

I would like to express my gratitude to Johanne, Anna, Fouzia, Ramez, Florence, Mary-Sylvie, Isabel, Michelle, Katy, Marquise, Jocelyne, and Diana for their exuberant generosity, inspiring ideas, extraordinary help, and amazing support in creating this dating odyssey to share among single souls on online dating sites. Also, I would like to thank my editor, Jon Goodman, from Manhattan, New York for his generous , advice, and comments—all of which enhanced my book, and pushed it into a professional publishing standard.

Readers' Comments

Before publishing my story, I got comments from randomly selected readers on the dating site Plenty of Fish (POF), as well as from some acquaintances. I wanted to confirm that my manner of presenting the events is respectful towards all women. Naturally, my angle is male, with a man's natural perspective and his raw emotions towards the opposite sex on online dating sites.

Out of 42 women selected for my study, 30 have deeply loved my writings, seven loved to read them, and one would prefer that this subject be written about by a woman. Four of the women were against it. So, 89% of the women who have read my work have approved of my style and my confessions as a man on this dating odyssey. Among them were 31 women who knew me only by my writing of this book.

Below is a selection of their comments. The first three are from professional authors:

Good evening André,

I think the content of your project is very interesting. I loved your descriptions of dating meetings and your expectations. Your writing is frank, straightforward and comforting. To sum it up, it is a great project and I sincerely believe that you have done a great job and it would be great if you could associate with someone who could help you with the publishing. I wish you the best of luck. Nat M.

Andre,

I can proudly state that Infinite Shades of Happiness is not like "50 Shades of Grey" or "Fire and Fury." It is not a controversial book, but it is a book about the search for love and I truly enjoyed reading it. I recommend it to others, especially those who are going through the digital dating life. Very well done. Sherrell N.

Hello André,

I find your book very entertaining. To be honest, I had mentally prepared myself for a boring read about what to do and not do. I think you were able to approach this subject in a very interesting way, and I found myself not only enjoying the story but hooked to it, which is important. I actually read until 2am last night because I really wanted to know how the Natalie story would unfold. Tânia G.

Hi André,

I read 45 pages in one go this morning. I found the text very interesting and entertaining. I liked that your writing can be read easily, as well as your storyline, which is between anonymous fiction and the reality of dating encounters. Gisèle N.

Hi André.

You made me laugh... I'm a filmmaker and I'm working on a similar project... Actually, very different, but on the same subject. I find your project interesting and I would like to talk to you about it further. But I will not do this in writing ... it's too long and complicated... writing sometimes lacks nuances, but not in your book by all means.

See you, Marquise L.

André...

Excuse me, I didn't have the time (or rather I didn't find the time to do only this! :)) ... I've just started and reading is pleasant. A book that you can read in the comfort of your bed sheets. It's a very light-hearted book, but deep at the same time. There are two messages: one of frivolity and one to read between the lines... It's nice and it's the good timing :)... Thank you ... Nath K!

Hello "dear" André!!!!

Wowww... I've read your literary essay. I feel that you've described very well the real world of dating sites, with the real texts we receive as participants (being insignificant most of the time, not touching our souls. Bravo for your courage.). Elena B.

Andre,

Like I said, I did like the book very much. I liked reading about a guy's point of view of dating from a dating site. I haven't read anything like that, so it was a new take on the guy's version of dating and getting the girl, so to speak. That was the hook that got me. Cristina S.

Hello André,

I truly enjoyed reading your book. I believe that it's incredibly well written and has the potential to help many women in the quest to achieve true happiness. Your use of humor throughout the story made for quite the entertaining and easy flowing read. I look forward to seeing your book published! -Stern M

Andre.

I think you can truly publish a great book. You had great lines and these lines kept me reading. You kept me laughing the entire way as well. It's not easy being humorous in stories, so well done. Magi. T.

Table of Contents

Introduction

This book was inspired by conversations with more than two hundred women who told me about their disappointment with men who seemed to misunderstand their motives for trying online dating sites. To better understand why so many men seemed to be missing the point, as well as to find a soul mate of my own, I decided to try online dating myself. What I learned – about me, about women, and about online dating – went far beyond anything I could ever have anticipated. To say it was an experience filled with twists, turns and surprises would be an understatement.

I do not intend to judge or discourage online dating, just to share my real-life experiences. My hope is to highlight the common mistakes and traps one can fall into when dating online. If I can accomplish that goal, maybe this book will help those who turn to dating sites – or even social media sites like Facebook or others – in a sincere effort to find a soul mate. I sure hope so because more and more people are using online dating sites every day.

The survey data gathered by Pew in June and July of 2015 were compared with data Pew gathered from a similar survey conducted in 2013. Online dating appears to have increased for almost every age group over the two years. – Forbes Magazine

This book is filled with surprises drawn from my dating encounters and includes stories intended to be entertaining to read as well as to share and discuss. The names of the individuals involved have necessarily been changed to protect their privacy, but as much as one may learn from the comments of the women who have graced this odyssey with their thoughts, so, too, will the discerning reader gain insight into the more subtle – and sensual – imaginings of the male mind.

You'll be able to follow my adventures as potential relationships progress from initial contacts through texts, emails and online chats, to face-to-face meetings and real-life dates. Along the way, you'll become familiar with my somewhat unorthodox writing style – what some people call my "Andréismes" — which are sometimes serious, sometimes humorous, but always honest and faithful to the reality of this dating world.

So, before making that commitment to venture into online dating, it is important to realize that all dating sites seem charming at first sight. They offer a wide range of opportunities, which could lead us to believe it is possible to change our lives. But, in reality, these online dating sites are only practical tools. They are Internet apps that facilitate virtual encounters and, perhaps, will lead to meetings in real life, and nothing more. There, your true challenge begins.

The situations you will read about include the kinds of offers you may receive as soon as you post your profile, some of which may leave you wondering, "Who *are* these people on dating sites?" It's no wonder so many women choose to cloak their true identity in their virtual profiles!

I tried my best to be objective when examining and questioning my actions after each of my dating experiences. I tried to show, honestly, the dimensions of one man's reasoning in a fair way. But just to keep me truly honest, and to maintain perspective, the comments of a range of women are included at the end of each chapter in the book. It's like a concept – he said, she said – but she has multiple faces, origins, ages and cultural backgrounds.

The search for love is universal and these women represent a range of countries and cultures from six continents, with an important North American presence, where online Internet dating sites were first created in 1990s. As I learned, online dating sites offer a wide range of opportunities to everyone but it is very easy to get lost. Close to fifty women who offered their comments helped me keep it real.

For some of them, English is a second or third language, so please give them the benefit of the doubt when it comes to the grammatical precision of their contributions. While my own words have been professionally edited, I did not wish to edit their comments with the same strict approach because to do so would rob many of the comments of their individual personality and flavour.

I believe, and I hope, that you will appreciate my stories. Taken as a whole, I think this book will deepen your knowledge of the insandouts (no pun intended) of virtual dating, and that you'll discover the true meaning of the old saying: "The journey of life is sometimes more important than the destination itself."

I'd like to complement this with my own metaphor:

The world of online dating encounters is like an infinite sky that surrounds us above and changes constantly. It can become black and cloudy, where thunderstorms and lightning threaten to strike at any moment. However, it will eventually clearup, as always, and benevolent breaks will become like nuances of happiness that we all deserve. Then, and finally, it is up to us, and only us, to recognize them truly, to seize them, to embrace them and, above all, to hold them for life.

CHAPTER 1

Happiness – Date to Inaugurate

The dawn emerges from the dark of night.

I am ready to launch into a fascinating adventure. I look to seize the hands of the woman I seek. I have never been so determined in my quest for happiness. And this? This looks promising. I do not think myself too old or too late; I deserve happiness and I am going to get it.

Sorry.

How rude of me.

Allow me to introduce myself: I am André.

Status: heterosexual, twice-divorced father of a beautiful teenage girl

Education: Graduate in civil engineering of "École Polytechnique de Montréal", McGill MBA, experienced senior executive in Canadian Fortune 100 companies

Thanks to mobile parents, I've lived in remarkable places. I've attended schools on three continents—in Warsaw, Poland, which was at the time part of the communist system in Eastern Europe. I was also schooled in Tunisia, in Northern Africa, before I got admitted for my baccalaureate in Paris, France. My final formal education took place in Montreal, in Quebec, Canada. Schooling in both French and English schools made me well versed in both languages. But it should come as no surprise that sometimes I feel confused by the multiple linguistic meanings dancing in my head.

I am the living proof of Einstein's theory of general relativity. This theory claims that the description of the same object or event observed from different places is influenced by the specificities of the place from which it is observed. Therefore, where is the absolute truth? Does it even exist, or does everything have a relative value, even the meaning of gender relationships? What a question! Did my continental migrations develop an enhanced acceptance of change? Will my international experiences help me find true love and succeed in my interpersonal "love" relationships? I'm not at all certain.

I celebrated my first marriage at the Mary-Reine-du-Monde Cathedral in Montreal with the personal blessing of Pope John Paul II. I owe my gratitude to my mother's relation to the Vatican— a Polish indigene.

My wife, whom I met at the campus of the University de Montreal, had a bachelor's degree in biology and was beginning her master's degree in medical biology when we married. At first, it was a match made in heaven: like cream complementing cheese. My wife was fun and loving. It was bliss, for a while. But as we rolled forth, like they say, "time spins off the finery."

With both of us caught up in our master's studies, we spent seven years without making growing our family a priority. Our studies absorbed us more than full time and brief leisure trips were our only breathing room. It was not until much later that we discussed children. I wanted children. She did not.

Realizing that professional ambition wasn't everything and that creating a family was important to me, I decided to start restructuring my life into what I was convinced was right. After twelve years of living together we had reached an impasse; it rang the death knell for our relationship.

My second relationship was solemnly built around the will to have children and build a family. With my second marriage, the purchase of a home, and the birth of our child, I was aiming to create the haven in which we wanted to raise our daughter.

Twelve years into my second marriage, although my wife and I had been able to raise our daughter and give her an education, our own union seemed burnt out. The spice, and all the flavour, had been lost. It was clear that there was an incompatibility in our characters that we couldn't fix. Contrary to the cliché about love relationships lasting three years, in my case, apparently, they last twelve. So, after a dozen years together, and more disappointment, it looked like I had wasted another good part of my life—except for the birth of our daughter. She was my only consolation.

I am now back at square one. And hence my presence now–after swearing to celibacy–in front of a computer screen struggling to fill out my profile on a dating site. This time, I hope my search for a soul mate results in the right one. I could, with some sarcasm, paraphrase my life like Calvin Harris sings in his video, *My Way*. Otherwise, time will pass like water under the bridge with no restraint.

- But what does the woman of my dreams look like?
- What qualities in a person am I looking for? What exactly do I even mean by that?
- Where do I begin? How do I begin?

I considered Einstein's theory for happiness, written in 1922 in the Imperial Hotel Tokyo:

- Where there's a will, there's a way;
- The true sign of intelligence is not knowledge but imagination;
- A calm and humble life will bring more happiness than the pursuit of success and the constant restlessness that comes with it;
- When you are courting a nice girl, an hour seems like a second. When you sit on a red-hot cinder a second seems like an hour. That's true relativity.

To be successful in my search, I've decided, I must keep these thoughts in mind. So, I'm off to begin my quest for happiness, my friends!

Dominique's angle
on the first chapter:

Is it really all relative, life perception?

I am Dominique from North Carolina, USA. I'm a 25-year-old woman still clinging to the vestiges of my youth. I'm running wild and traveling the world in search of true, unadulterated happiness (if such a thing truly exists).

I graduated high school a year earlier than my peers. I immediately jumped into college life where I earned a BA in Creative Writing: my one true passion. In fact, writing was so important to me that I set aside many years for that sole pursuit, denying myself romantic involvements of any sort.

Further down the line, I realized I wanted to find and add that indescribable love of my life. I fully believed in true love (even love at first sight). Perhaps I'm a romantic at heart, but I don't want to believe there is anything less than that in the world.

That being said, I've also travelled a lot. I still travel and am travelling even as I write this. Like André, I've seen some remarkable places and met many remarkable people. It is so very true that Einstein's theory of relativity is alive and proven in this world. Everything is influenced by the specificities of the place from which it is observed, including the pursuit and definition of love.

I believe there is an absolute truth and that truth, however you boil it down, is simply love. There may be extraneous factors in the relative definitions of gender relationships, but love is universal.

So why couldn't I find it?

It's a possibility that all my travelling left me drifting in my pursuit of love, while more stable people developed a solid foundation upon which to find love?

Like André, I eventually turned to the option of online dating. Sitting at a computer screen completing ridiculous profiles and compatibility quizzes, I had the hope that somewhere in the universe there was someone who was just as confused about how to find love as I was.

They say you never find love when you are seeking it, but I've never been one to wait for things to happen to me. I was determined to make this search fruitful and serious, so I asked myself questions very similar to André's:

- What does the man of my dreams look like?
- What qualities and personality traits am I looking for?
- How do I have the patience to wade through the hundreds and millions that don't meet my standards?
- Should I even have standards?

When entering the world of online dating, I'm sure these are thoughts that cross almost everyone's mind. The online dating world of today is just as relative as real world dating. Connections and communications are relative to the platforms used: Tinder, POF, Bumble, Match, etc. They all have different rules and standards, just like if I were dating in Tokyo and then went to Brazil. The difference can be that drastic.

I never found love online. I made connections, lost connections, put in too much effort or not enough effort, but it was all part of the process of finding love. For some people, the journey may end online. For others, it is only a stepping stone in the dating world.

Again, it's all relative.

Lin Rose's angle on the first chapter:

Online dating is for true grown-ups.

> "A True Grownup is a person that can pitch and barter him/herself as a valuable online product."

Hello, my name is Lin Rose. I'm at the age of 29 from Xiamen City in mainland China. I have one Canadian parent and have lived some time in UK . I am now living in China. I am glad to contribute with a Chinese woman's perspective to André's dating odyssey.

Love! I think finding and keeping love in today's world is now more head-wracking than ever, even for a woman in a country with the largest human population in the world. The hope that the situation will get any better is rather bleak.

I am a Chinese woman, and I say this with pride. I am woman who grew up hearing stories of how my parents and their friends found love in festivals, during family visits, and practically at any point of physical contact. An enticing culture this author wished was still in wide practice. I must admit that we partake in some of the same nostalgia.

The internet did change the dating game.

Every time I hear the phrase "online-dating," I think of e-commerce. This upsets my stomach terribly. It requires that a person gets the specifics correct and providing essential personal data, even if the chance to ever find love is not guaranteed. The product (in this case, a human being) must promote itself properly and in a seducing manner.

Here in China, e-commerce service providers give sellers the opportunity to pitch their products to potential buyers. Basically, there are two groups of people on the website: the sellers and the buyers.

But online dating is very much complicated. Every profile is a product trying to sell itself and equally on the lookout for a product to buy– fair exchange. The crucial criterion is in your pitching skills.

I must say, this takes us back centuries into the ice age, when people had to barter products as a means of livelihood.

Carolina's angle
on the first chapter:

Where do I begin and how do I begin?

I am a French woman in my late twenties from Paris, France. I have witnessed multiple divorces in my family and circle of friends so André's questions in this chapter are more than pertinent.

Considering a new relationship after a divorce is a challenge, but you need to cool off your internal fires. You need to feel good about yourself and to be lucid. You need to relax, laugh with your pals and get out! You should definitely preserve yourself to avoid getting paralyzed by doing some sport. Your frame of mind and thoughts regarding life before considering dating is a key component for your future happiness. Preserving a clean head and heart is a healthful thing. If you consider these suggestions, you will have higher chances of success in dating after a divorce.

Here are practical suggestions to consider after divorce:

Seek help from a buddy or your own family:

Any withdrawing from your family or close friends could be extremely painful. If you can get it, trusted support is essential after your divorce to prevent you from feeling alone. But, choose cautiously those whom you lean on.

Participate in a support institution:

An option is to get help from organizations designed to help you after divorce. You can connect with other fellows in similar conditions to yours and listen to how they're coping. This may be particularly useful in the case your divorce ended in an uncongenial manner. This includes abuse, addiction, or infidelity. Search for divorce agencies like Divorce Care.

Make new friends:

Many people will find that after a marriage, the landscape of their social circle will change. You and your spouse may have shared pals who now may pick to remain close to one of you rather than both of you. Old buddies may not be as interested to see you because of your changed social status. You may need to search for new friendships.

Start to date only when you're ready:

Dating is difficult after a divorce. My sincere advice is to avoid dating for a minimum of three months, but I often see that a one-year period works best for some people. It is absolutely your decision. The only recommendation I have is to not take yourself too seriously, and to try not to look for "the only one" as an immediate goal. No one wants to date a guy who spontaneously cries, who complains too much, or who talks continuously about his ex-spouse. You need to establish meaningful expectations for dating before going out.

Natasha's angle on the first chapter:

Love is within reach of a keyboard.

I'm Natasha, a twenty-five-year-old married woman living in Melbourne, Australia. My husband is forty-two and at the moment, we don't have children. I work for a Spanish editorial company, which fits with my hobby: traveling. In spite of knowing too many people around the world, I never could find someone to love while on my life-path. So, in 2014, I decided to create an account on an online-dating site.

At the beginning, I was irritated because I had to answer idiotic (and repetitive) questions to describe myself to my ideal fellow. The last question was the most difficul for met: how do you know who would be "the man?" He would not necessarily be like me, nor my antithesis.

I am a writer and I opted to write a lot on my profile. Anyway, no one read it; they only chatted with me to say stupid things. Never will be absent that one who thinks he is a powerful seducer, who is sold as the jackpot, or who introduces his resume. Months passed by and my search results were getting better. Finally, I found the right person to chat with: his name is Tim.

We connected daily for a year until we agreed to meet face to face. I felt anxious to talk to him, to touch him, to feel him, in real life. I was excited even to discover his fragrance. I remember that night before our first meeting, I couldn't sleep because I couldn't stop thinking about our first date. I made a list in my mind: check the traffic, order a taxi early in the morning, choose topics for the conversation, select possible answers, and com-bine clothes. At that moment, I got out of bed. I kept awake that night.

Heading out to our meeting place, I got nervous. The fear that he could not be real invaded me, and for an instant, I wanted to go back home. I felt a horrible pressure in my stomach. I felt the need to throw up in the taxi. But it was too late for regrets. I convinced myself that "if he does not show up, it would not have to be the end of the world."

Fortunately, everything went very well once Tim came to meet me. We already knew each other, but it didn't matter because we talked a lot. Tim didn't (and doesn't) see life in the same way as me, but we still share the same interests.

Today I am glad to say that after another year, Tim married me. Now, we both enjoy traveling together. Tim has what I want in a man: sincerity, an honest heart, charm, and above all, intelligence.

In this century, it is not easy establish contact with a stranger, so I am sure that online dating helps many to take the first step. Also, I believe the fact of not knowing if the photo or economic position presented are real gives the advantage of knowing the real person through the words. Starting with an online "friend" is a great way to find true love.

Helen's angle
on the first chapter:

Be yourself and know what you want.

I am Helen, a thirty-seven-year-old single-mother of a beautiful daughter. I have a B.Sc. in Communication Studies from Eastern University, USA. I am moved by challenges and changes happening around me. I am a professional writer with eight years of writing experience. I strongly believe in finding love, and I also love to see the good in people irrespective of ethnicity. But, I do (like any other woman) have a sense of personal taste.

There are many reasons why a person would choose to date online rather (or in addition to) dating in person. After all, online dating is based on your own schedule, and can be as personal or impersonal as you would like.

When dating online, it's important to look at the whole process as more of a casual one rather than as a potential, actual soulmate connection. Online dating will take time, sometimes as much (if not more) time than actual person-to-person dating. Just as in an offline relationship, things may simply not work out. This is my personal belief. I don't take most profile descriptions to be true, and I rarely go through them.

During my quest for true love, I lived in Alaska. I loved the Alaskan environment as well as the weather. However, I was also looking for anyone who lived in other parts of the United States. I met someone who lived in Maryland, and we would talk on the phone for hours. I loved the sound of his voice, and his sense of humor. Considering that our internet service was via a high-speed connection, our relationship development was high-speed too!

I visited him in Maryland the first weekend in July. My parents and friends were concerned that he could be an "axe-murderer." Of course, after talking to him on the phone as many hours as I did, I knew he was someone I could trust. At the end of July, he came to Alaska and proposed that same month. We were married in Maryland in October of the same year. Talk about a whirlwind romance!

Some people ask: "Well, how'd you get to know him so well?" When you only have the phone, it is very easy. Think about face-to-face dates. Sometimes, you are playing miniature golf, watching a movie, or doing other things that do not involve talking.

We only could talk! So, it allowed us to really get to know each other. It did not last a lifetime, though, and that got me back to the POF date site. Only you know what you are looking for. Don't settle for less than who you want. Believe in your ability to get just the right partner.

Online dating may be the perfect way to find them!

Luna's angle
on the first chapter:

What is true dating?

My name is Luna from Louisville, USA. I am a twenty-five-year-old woman with no children. For the last fourteen months I've been dating a 'best friend-turned-boyfriend'. I have an MSN and work as a Nurse Practitioner. I absolutely love my job and I feel like I'm actually helping people! Despite this, I still feel a strong wanderlust, so I make sure to travel every chance I get. As a result, I traveled home to Germany a few times to visit family, and I plan to travel to Romania or Mexico very soon.

I grew up in Germany. When I was nine, my parents moved us to the USA. Due to my father's job, we moved around quite frequently and I went to many different schools. I met a lot of people through this, let's say, both good and bad. This continued until I graduated high school.

I experimented with dating a bit after this and only two of the relationships developed into anything serious. At the time, I was afraid of agreeing to a relationship and getting stuck with the "wrong" guy. Most of my boyfriends turned out to be sexually active, while I was not. After noticing the overwhelming amount of stress this caused, I decided to just take a complete break from the dating scene to just worry about putting my own happiness first.

Fast forward a few years and my childhood best friend asked me out during a gathering with friends. I'm very happy in this relationship and don't feel pressured at all. I think the key to a healthy relationship is mutual respect and understanding. I firmly believe that there is someone out there for everyone. Every time I did online dating, I absolutely loved the experience. It felt natural, and for the most part, rather carefree. I was completely blind to the true intentions of some people. I didn't know how to really read between the lines of texts and online profiles. It's always important to know exactly what boundaries you want to set for yourself, and for your potential love interest.

André does an amazing job of describing how a functional relationship should be. I certainly wish I had this book when I was just starting out dating, as I had absolutely no clue!

Clara's angle on the first chapter:

Without any ambiguity.

Hi, I am Clara: a European first name but with genuine African roots. I am twenty-six-years old, never been married and I have a diploma in performing arts from Obafemi Awolowo University in Ile-Ife, plus a BSc in Mass Communications from the National Open University in Africa. I fully believe in finding love and I also love to see the good in people no matter what they have done or what they do. So, no matter how messy and painful a break up is, I like to move on to the next best thing.

My first relationship lasted six years. We were together since high school till my second year in the University. I was sixteen and he was twenty. Yes, there was a four-year difference. The truth is when he first asked me out, he thought I was eighteen because my body was like that of an eighteen to twenty-year-old girl: my bust was already a 34D, my hips were 38 inches, and my waist was 20. I had an hourglass shape which made older guys come after me.

Me being me, I also never liked guys my age because I felt they were immature. When we started dating, he was sexually active and I was not. I also wasn't ready because of my personal belief and also wanting it to be perfect. At first, he was okay with it and never pressured me for sex. We loved each other, and that was enough. Three years into the relationship, I was 19 and he felt I was old enough to have sex, but I turned him down. I just wasn't ready. I noticed he started having one-night stands with other girls.

Three years later, I still wasn't ready. We broke up.

My second relationship was a year later when I was 24. At first, I was scared to get into another relationship because I thought sex was going to be required from me often, but my new boyfriend was great. He was a bodybuilder and work-out instructor and was very sensitive. I felt very safe with him at all times and the connection was just great. We were attracted to each other sexually, but it wasn't a priority. He was six years older and was very mature. When sex happened, it just did and it was perfect.

A year later, we started to talk of marriage and that was when the plane crashed. We both had the same genotype, AS, which causes sickle cell anemia. He didn't care and he told me things would work out, and we could adopt. But I wanted my own kids and I didn't want to bring a child to the world to suffer from that devastating disease. I was in a dilemma, to choose my perfect man now, then suffer later, or to continue my search for my soulmate. I chose the latter and we broke up. It was so painful to lose a good man.

For me, I didn't feel like I wasted my time or years as I actually gained something. Relationships, good or bad, teach you one thing or the other. You learn how to do things different. With this in mind, the question is, "What do I want in a man?"

My Perfect Man

I acknowledge that there is no perfect person, so by "perfect man," I mean a man with attributes that meet my topmost needs.

On the top of the list is:

Sincere Man: A man who is not scared to tell me the truth, even if it hurts me. A man who is not pretentious.

Good Communicator: a guy who listens and pays attention to my non-verbal communication. A kind, responsible, but also daring and adventurous man. He must also be mature — not only physically, but emotionally. A guy who is not self-centered.

Good Looks: I don't care about race, nationality, or color. I want a guy who is at least 5ft6 inches, physically fit, and who cares about his all-round hygiene. An ambitious guy who knows what he wants in life.

So, let's begin!

Katia's angle on the first chapter:

Online and offline dating, what a combination!

Hi! I'm Katy, a young woman from a recently created country called Georgia. I'm a twenty-three-year-old master's student at a university in Malta who has been in a very long-distance relationship with dating in general. You might think: "How does that work?" Quite easy.

If you were me, who was raised in a post-Soviet Union country in a quite liberal family, you would have your own views on life. My family (who I love a lot) believes they have to be much, much better than any other family in my country (they have given me a lot). But while the average American or European teenager starts getting interested in dating, instead, when I was 17, I was focused on studying to achieve some superb milestones and I completely disregarding any type of a love life.

Oh, I wasn't one of those who didn't know how babies came or how sex worked. Nope. If I wanted information, the internet, books, and theoretical knowledge were sufficient for me. However, soon (in university), I started to see that everyone else was dating, online, offline, or both at the same time. Then there was me: I had a life plan which did not include any serious relationships at all. But for superficial relationships, I was ready. Just on my own terms.

But I doubt you are reading this to know the sorry state of my love life right now. You want to get a glimpse into a real-life event that happened to me. Ready?

Online dating… Always knew about it, tried it. Tinder appeared on my phone once, but I deleted it a few hours later after realizing that my idea of guys was correct, and the only thing they wanted from me was sex. Sorry—I thought as I hit the delete button—not getting it that easily. I never got completely into it.

So, I tried chatting for some time, but I was spending too much time with my studies and didn't get into that either.

Thus, my online dating has ended for now. I'll just go back to travelling and reading books. As my best friend says: "You have time before You," so I keep doing whatever I am doing.

And for those who are still searching for their second half, keep searching. Just be sure to know who you are talking to!

Niki's angle
on the first chapter:

A Vintage Love in the Modern Age

I was born in Rabat, Morocco, beside a magnificent ocean's beach. I've always longed to be from a different time, another era, one which thrives upon love in its most beautiful form. But being a nineties kid, I had to grow up into a world in which people are racing themselves, greedy and in constant search of intimacy and emotion, even if it was as temporarily as one's admiration for a new toy. I swore to never be caught up in the game, but I failed to keep that promise. After reading Andrés online dating story, it reminded me of my own experience, which I'd like to share as a reply. My story is like a modernized fairy-tale: the impossible coming true, as two people from different countries, races, and backgrounds fell in love.

So, as you see, my experience is not quite a one date story. It's about love manifesting as a great power, which eliminated all differences and brought up all similarities. But what's the most outstanding to me is when I was following the wave, racing and searching for my prince charming, I was hit by disappointments and dust. However, when I stopped wandering around with my heart on display, love came looking for me in the most unusual place. Out of nowhere, the utmost cliché happene: He commented on an online post, so I replied. He sent me a friend request, so I accepted. And now we're engaged. It seems so simple, yet so complicated to achieve emotionally. We didn't exchange pictures. He didn't ask, and neither did I. It drove us towards each other in a unique way.

In the beginning, we were just friends, and then we became good friends. We shared our weird sense of humor together and slowly, we were unfolding each other. We were getting rid of all the masks and wrecking down the protection walls that our damaged souls built in a moment of self-resurrection, after daggers of betrayal and disappointment were stabbed right in our hearts. He wasn't the arrogant, careless, and immature person I thought him to be, and my heart wasn't as dead as it seemed. On a rainy night, I was sitting by my bed looking through the window. The sky was gloomy, but lights of dawn started to appear, and traces of a new day were becoming clearer. It was so quiet and peaceful, I could hear no other sound but the rain pouring on the window. Then, I suddenly jumped when my phone rang. My heart was beating so fast. I sneaked a peak on the glowing screen, and it was him. I picked up.

"I couldn't sleep" he stated the obvious, with his husky sleepy voice, which always seemed to send an electric feel down my spine.

"Why?" His breathing pattern got heavier as I asked.

"Your voice is so beautiful" his voice didn't express sleepiness this time; on the contrary, he seemed wide awake.

"You know, I didn't plan this, and I don't know what to say, or in matter of fact, I do know exactly what to say, but... I... I can't keep it within me anymore, I have to tell you." His voice was shaky. He was scared, of the unknown, of the reaction. He feared regret, which he might have to deal with for the rest of his life if his decision happens to ruin the unique feelings we already shared.

"What do you mean?" I asked, knowing what he means. But in that moment, I didn't know anything.

"I have feelings for you, I didn't plan this, I'm sorry."

Suddenly, I got hit by different emotions. I was overwhelmed, scared, excited, but I knew that I had the same feelings for him. Still, I just froze.

"What do you mean? Are you joking? Is this a joke to you?" I replied.

"I love you." He stated in a clear voice. Suddenly, he wasn't shaky. He was confident; he believed in what he said. And being the stone hearted, cold-blooded woman that I always claimed to be, I burst into tears.

"I love you too." I replied. I was shaking, crying, laughing, and hardly breathing. But I didn't doubt our feelings. Not even once. I blindly trusted him even through being the woman who trusted no one. I loved him truly with all I have, even though I was the woman who swore to never fall in love, to never be a part of the modern age with all its trends and technologies. And he loved me with all our differences, though he is the man who never believed in love eliminating the strongest boundaries.

We, with no doubt, changed for the better. I am currently smiling as I'm typing these words. And I am very glad I gave myself a chance to be a part of the modern age. Although I kept my vintage vibe, leading to the contraries of giving birth to the most beautiful, life changing experience I never thought I'd be lucky enough to have.

Nour's angle
on the first chapter:

Online love and cultural restrictions?

I am Nour from Cairo, Egypt. I am twenty-two years old, and I like designing, music, art, and movies. I'm a slightly romantic person, and I overthink/imagine my life from very different perspectives. Every night, I imagine myself in a new romantic story with my dream guy, or the perfect position at work. I don't have many friends. I only have some from my old school who don't talk to me much. There are others from my college that I would call mates. But only one best friend, who used to travel a lot, so we didn't have much time to spend together. That's why I spend most of my time on the internet. I like chatting more than talking or face to face communication. It's like I'm too shy to talk or react in real life, so I choose to live all that behind my laptop. Sometimes I choose nicknames for myself when I'm talking to someone new, which makes me feel more comfortable. I don't search very much for love, but just simple company.

One day, I heard about a website which you could meet up with people all around the world. I made an account in a minute with a nickname. I was really excited to see what was going to happen on this website. Once I clicked the online button, many people started chatting with me. People talk about everything with each other. We all shared funny images of animals. At first, I didn't feel comfortable talking to them, so I would just watch their conversations without replying.

But suddenly, a name came up and got my attention for no reason. Maybe because it was an Arabic name? I opened the chat, started talking to him, and he was really nice to me. He didn't flirt too much like other guys on private messages. Bilal is my new friend from an awkward website that lives so far away from Egypt. He's not Arabic, but he just has an Arabic name. I liked a guy with a foreign language, different traditions, life style, and skin color. But I admit: He has his own charm that appears from some words through a keyboard. We got used to each other. We would spend weeks talking every day for a long time about many random topics, and about ourselves without getting bored. We started video calls, we got into a relationship and we didn't even notice it coming.

So, we shared our feelings with a forging language. None of us could talk the other's language, or even understand it (and it is really tough not knowing when we'd meet in real or touch each other), but only our souls did. We were always online, holding our cellphones everywhere we went. This period of my life took so long. I knew it wouldn't work till the end.

I live in an Arabic country, which may have some problems getting married to a foreign guy. But I couldn't run until I realized I was only dreaming of this. A dream which couldn't've be true, I would cry myself to sleep. I was suffering from not meeting him, and I was too young to get enough money to visit him. But I ran from him without looking back again, and it was so hard for me. He said he'd do anything to stay with me and fix those little silly problems. But I chose the easiest way to live. I'd wait for the right easy love which wouldn't make any trouble. How silly I was for throwing away such a true love.

CHAPTER 2

First Steps – Why Not Me?

It was on the Plenty of Fish (POF) dating site that two of my best friends found the heart of their lives. I am aware that this expression—"heart of their lives"—probably does not really exist. It's one of the "Andréismes" I mentioned in the introduction, and considering English is a living language, homologation by the Merriam-Webster Dictionary of the term "Andréisme" could always follow later.

If it worked for my friends, why wouldn't it work for me? I often consult my friends and take their advice. Although the world of virtual dating has thrown me into an unfamiliar dimension of modern romance, I still feel I can immerse myself in it if I get enough courage, though I must admit everything looks new to me.

Let's be frank. Without any shame, I can say that I do not know about virtual dating or its rules. In the old times, everything happened in a bar or at a social gathering. A search for a suitable candidate would be carried out among the members of the opposite sex who were physically present.

We could see every lady and their charm, admire their movements, realize their natural vivacity, anticipate their lure, let ourselves be conquered by their sex appeal, test our own, and finally, the ultimate bliss, speak to them. And the most fascinating part, coming last but not least, was hearing the timbre of their unique voice, the signature of their personality.

How I miss it all now, this loss of physical dating, that we are replacing with the new concept called online dating. Therefore,

I'm referring to the "virtual"world as though it were a definite place on Earth, but I'm sure we all know that it rarely is.

So, for any science nerds reading, here's a metaphor. Online dating is like a virtual quasi-principality, outside of physical reality in three dimensions that is governed by rules and dogmas of its own. We must adapt and behave accordingly.

So, it is in front of a screen that we must guess the dimensions and physical appeal of our desired Romeos and Juliets. A Herculean task! Charms and potential love compatibilities, as well as photos and profile descriptions, are the first and only tools for selecting one's date. Nothing else. It seems we have to get accustomed to it, as this is apparently the new "natural" way to meet single people in today's society. Good God, I don't want to sink into nostalgia for the past, but I already miss the good old days. I can still smell and remember them.

Whatever the case is in dating today, let's stay positive. It can't get any worse, can it? And so I decide to take the first step, which is filling out my profile on the Plenty of Fish site. I don't want to be alone anymore. So first, I need to move in the right direction and choose my nickname—my username. This choice should pique the opposite sex's curiosity.

I like music, so let's try a neutral option like Vivaldi17, a combination of the name of a known and rather baroque composer who inspires romantic impulses in the opposite sex. Add the day of my birth to it and the first step is done.

As for my age, I must admit that Mother Nature has been generous when it comes to my face and physiognomy. No one can guess my age. Without being pretentious, I'm staying realistic about myself. So, one point to me in this beauty contest between genders.

Here's how the process goes. Writing simple lines, I still spent more than two hours hesitating. Once my profile is complete, I have to admit that this quest looks very promising … but will it deliver my happiness?

VIVALDI17

Motto of the profile:	Have you met your soulmate?
Details:	Vintage years old, Male, 6 feet 2 inches (188 cm)
City:	Montréal
Profession:	Professional
Education:	Master's Degree
Smokes?	No
Has children?	Yes
Personality:	Open-minded
Looking for:	Woman
For:	Serious relationship
Family situation:	Divorced
Race:	Caucasian
Drinks alcohol?	Socially
Figure:	Normal
Animals:	No
Second language:	French
Does drugs?	No
Hair:	Blond
Eye color:	Blue
Has a car:	Yes
Astrological sign:	Virgo
Wants kids?	No
Longest relationship:	More than 10 years
Are you ambitious?	Yes

DESCRIPTION

- Like you, I guess I am looking for a serious and long-term relationship. My hobbies are cooking, going to the cinema, and feeding my soul with good music.
- I consider myself a very authentic person in today's demanding social world, where norms are constantly evolving, and recognize a multitude of social beliefs.

- Moreover, I think I am very well developed and properly groomed, relationally.
- I actively keep myself in shape, physically and mentally.

ASSUMPTIONS

- For me, the key to a healthy relationship is to keep an open mind, to value and show respect for our differences, and accept our imperfections above all. Being honest and respectful is the foundation of my life.
- To me, patience is a paramount virtue, just like sense of humour. A mixture of both will give an almost perfect partner.
- And if you share those beliefs about life, you are welcome to join me in my living space.

At noon I am satisfied with my presentation. Next, I'll be choosing my profile picture, one wherein I smile and look casual, but not neglected. Women are intuitive when they look at pictures. I have to maximize my chances.

Once my profile is complete, I upload my data, including my photo, on POF. One hour and fifteen minutes later, I get my first message:

On April 7th – 1:15 p.m. Lessens69 wrote:

Is it above all a search for a relationship or to share human pleasure?

Thank you for enlightening me.

Cynthia

Damn it! Did she even read my profile, or did she simply look at my picture? The description on my profile seems clear to me. I'm sure even Stevie Wonder could've seen better than she had. I dash off to view her profile and get myself a punch in the face; I am flabbergasted by her posted description:

"Needs for the calm of large spaces or the activity of great centers. Sometimes, being a morning person and sometimes, lingering. Capable of moving a lot of air or great idleness, I sometimes like the two facets of the same reality.

Interested in a guy that's not too perfect, perfection often being very boring, with whom to share our energies and the little things of life in order to live happy and spicy moments or sadder moments if the imagination does not follow."

Yes, life is not fair for everyone. Certainly, it hasn't been fair to me, and Cynthia reserves her right to seek happiness, notwithstanding. But the day one decides to appear on dating sites is the day they must swallow their pride and allow their spirit to be positive, maybe inflated with optimism.

Succeeding in "faking" some life joy and sharing it with others is the minimum requirement. But talking about boredom and sadness is a complete turn-off. You should caution yourself to stay away from such ignominy, preserving yourself and your personal worth. Ask yourself these basic questions:

- Are we not looking to seduce a future partner for life, rather than chase them away?
- Or could they be sending a coded message that requires deciphering?

Her description does not appeal to me in any way. No allure, and no spice; maybe too honest and not enough magic?

But I still believe that Cynthia, as resigned and negative as her profile has established her to be, deserves my respectful reply. Staying respectful is my driving force in life. I don't want to deal a blow to her self-esteem, or inadvertently reveal what I think of her.

So, I choose an answer based on physical compatibility, which is, I think, a universal and indisputable concept. Then, I start writing my reply. Keep in mind that people's responses are often reactive and sometimes insecure, but we have to try and perhaps gain some satisfaction. Will she be happy and serene? We'll see.

April 7th – 2:24 p.m. Vivaldi17 wrote:

Thank you, Cynthia, for your message. I visited your profile. As you know, the goal of an approach on this site is to recognize a mutual physical attraction.

However, I don't think it's the case here, for me at least.

Sincerely, Andre

April 7th – 2:34 p.m. Lessens69 wrote:

Thanks, Andre. Very honest reply from you.

Good luck! Cynthia

A few minutes later and—already!—another message pops up. This time, forget the tissues and the tears to the eyes. Be a man in flesh and blood.

April 7th – 2:45 p.m. Betty50 wrote:

Hi

April 7th – 2:46 p.m. Vivaldi17 wrote:

Hello, Betty50

April 7th – 2:47 p.m. Betty50 wrote:

No, I haven't met my soulmate yet.

April 7th – 2:48 p.m. Betty50 wrote:

In which sector do you work? Busy?

April 7th – 2:49 p.m. Vivaldi17 wrote:

I am cruising toward retirement – [typing quickly to keep pace]

April 7th – 2:50 p.m. Betty50 wrote:

The best occupation then.

April 7th – 2:51 p.m. Betty50 wrote:

Young civil servant?

April 7th – 2:52 p.m. Betty50 wrote:

I'm letting you be, it seems I'm annoying you, have a good day.

I barely had time to read her profile and she'd already flown to another planet in the virtual dating universe. I sincerely wish for her to find a man capable of following her, if such a man exists.

A second thought crossed my mind, and I could've been more patient, but hey, just because I'm retired doesn't mean I have time to waste with this frivolous "Speedy Gonzales" person. I hope my future messages will be more serene and serious.

Like a balm to my heart, two other messages slide through from Lilly1920 and Airelle007. I take my time to breathe, unable to steady myself. Finally, I catch my breath and hope, maybe, that I will not be thrown off the wagon by the speed of messages, or even the act in itself, as I experienced in the massive attack of Betty's emails.

We men are perhaps slower than women initially, but we catch up. I still hope these early experiences aren't representative of what's to come in my online dating life. But before anything else goes awry, let's play some music. I have always enjoyed the soothing capabilities of music, and I choose what I listen to withgreat care. Music provides me with low-cost therapy and helps me vent frustrations.

In this troubled moment, I relax, because only then can I think clearly and right. To let go of the anxiety, I set my sights on the lyrics of Adele's song "When We Were Young."

Soon, my mood seems afloat again and I am relaxed and comforted. I have hope again. Thanks, Adele, your music works for me. I'm ready to seek new adventures. I'm interested in Lilly1920's and Airelle007's messages, and a good reply is required! Despite the early missteps I'm truly satisfied and filled with joy at the beginning of my dating odyssey.

Lev's angle
on the 2nd chapter:

Writing profile has a link with physical attraction?

I am now a woman in my late 20's who grew up in rural New Jersey. The countryside was so beautiful there, but it was in that beautiful coutryside that I learned the sometimes-ugly truths about human nature and interactions, too.

Choosing a profile photo is perhaps the most critical element of your dating portfolio. This may seem harsh, and it is, because no one likes being assessed solely upon their physical attributes. We know ourselves to be more than the construction of our faces, or the contours of our waistlines, so reducing the unique vibrancy of our personalities to a mere snapshot can feel shallow to the point of folly.

Shouldn't personality be more important than attractiveness? Why does a stranger need to see your face in order to see your heart?

I empathize with these questions, but like Andre, I understand the necessity of physical chemistry. Selecting a mate is different than selecting a friend; there must be an element of sexual attraction between two people, a spark to light the wick, or else nothing intimate can transpire. Mother Nature has programmed us to seek out certain characteristics — both in personality and in appearance — and I don't see any sense in denying these inclinations. We have them for a reason, even if we do not consider the survival of our genes to be the most important priority in our lives.

However, while physical attraction may be a necessary ingredient, we must also fall in love with each other's personalities. What good is it to love your partner's looks, but not their thoughts? We would be better off pinning the pages of a Victoria's Secret catalogue to the bedroom wall rather than pursuing a relationship with an incompatible person, because such a relationship will no doubt end in disappointment. This is why it is so important that your profile reflects who you are.

Andre speaks wisdom on this point: if our profiles describe us accurately, then we can avoid the unnecessary disappointment of meeting our dates in person, feigning well-mannered conversation, then ending the evening with rejection. Honesty is a far better strategy.

If physical attractiveness matters, how may you maximize it? This is no mystery: eat well, work out, and care for your body like the temple it is. When choosing your profile picture, select a well-lit, friendly photograph that displays your best attributes, but is not artificially em-bellished. Smile, and don't slouch.

Remember that even if one person does not find you attractive, there are plenty of other people out there who will. Everyone likes something different, and no matter how short you are, what color hair you have, or what the girth of your waistline is, someone out there is waiting to meet someone just like you.

Leanne's angle
on the 2nd chapter:

A truly innocent British critique.

What I find funny about the dating scene is the sheer amount of pretense involved. It goes like this: "Hi, my name is 'Lord Lady.' it's an upper-class joke, but my friends call me Lee. I am in my early twenties, live in London, Great Britain, and I'm a passionate writer. These are the reasons that I should shag you.

People talk about online dating like it's different from the bygone days of old they so desperately yearn for. Where the man in the bar approaches the woman, he would least mind waking up next to, and announcing he has an imaginary, early meeting. But in truth, online dating has simply streamlined the process. Here are my intentions, my likes and dislikes, and the best photo of myself I can find. Can I shag you now?

I've never had the type of looks that drew a room's attention. I have a plain face, or so a lover once told me. I didn't really get messages on POF (Plenty of Fish), until I updated my profile to say: "I was just looking for someone with which to 'smoke Kush and chill', so maybe my judgement is clouded by my youth." But I can't help but conclude: people who seek love actively, rather than simply seeking a bond and waiting to see what develops, are naive and doomed to fail. The pressure on the other person to not be perfect – because no one would admit to wanting that – but to be worthy of your love, is too much. The relationship buckles before it's really, even begun. But not in 100% of cases, and I suppose that's what gives people hope.

The task at hand is a response, and here it is in full: the narrator is a laughable character. Now bear in mind, I say this as though I didn't suffer from the same affliction. However, I can't help but find it funny. The way he jumps, from the humbling hesitance of being new to the online dating scene, to thinking he knows enough, to critique people's profiles, within the space of an hour and fifteen minutes.

The woman's (Cynthia) profile looked to me like a spectacular show of honesty, with more than enough 'sparkle.' But that's just my opinion… and here's a little more. He was too quick to judge her on the basis that her reality did not match his. But with that said, I don't imagine the two would have been a good match. Her being more of a free spirit (or at least that's the vibe I got), and him being so deeply lodged in his own arse.

I once read an article that said: "the people you find the most annoying are the ones that remind you of yourself, in ways you don't like." So, maybe my venom toward the narrator shows more about me, than it does about him. Perhaps, the reason why I find it so easy to criticize his self-involvement is because it's a trap I can easily see myself falling into.

Yael's angle
on the 2nd chapter:

Online profile and Middle East mentality.

I'm Yael. I'm 26 years old from Tel Aviv, and I found love with online dating. In Israel (where I come from), online dating is popular in some circles. However, it's perceived as 'lame.' Why? It's either considered too sex-driven, or too low and not 'classy' enough for most people. Even in Tel Aviv, the most liberal city in Israel, online dating is considered one of the two above. Israel is a small country, and everyone kind of knows everyone. Therefore, the first question one would wonder about your online profile (and perhaps not to your face) is, 'Is it really SO hard for you to find someone? You're smart, attractive, successful - this is too desperate.' No one wants to be that someone.

But after a long while dating, truly desperate to find someone to feel natural with, I've finally decided to do it (secretly, of course, praying hard that no one I know would see my profile, ever). I've made my first online dating profile on 'OK Cupid', a popular online dating site which is considered decent in Israel. I was so afraid of looking like someone who tries too hard. I chose a casual photo, wore a big smile, wrote some random notes about myself — and waited.

A few minutes later, dozens of messages came through. By the time I answered, 10 new messages came in. After only a single day after posting my profile, I had 300 messages waiting for me from hundreds of men. Guess what? I answered ALL of them. Feeling wanted, being flattered and getting constant requests to meet is addictive. You just want to continue giving the audience what they want! There's a sense of betterment, superiority, and of course, confidence.

Online dating apps provide a platform where people feel comfortable just reaching out to you, because hey — we're here for the same purpose right? Why would I feel rejected here? How could I? And even if I do, they won't remember me anyways.

Andre's perspective reveals the real desire that everyone holds: feeling loved and wanted, getting noticed and desired, and finally, finding love that lasts. So really, who cares? Who cares if online dating is not as sexy and vibrant as meeting someone outside of the web? Who cares about society norms (which should always be questioned and challenged)? Who cares if someone thinks online dating is lame, when it might be the path leading you one step closer to finding your better half?

In this story (my own story), online dating made me gain back confidence I lacked from not dating. Finally, I've come to realize that all pathways towards love are equal, free from judgment and prejudice, online and offline. Getting noticed by so many men that found me attractive, both outside and inside, gave me the confidence I needed to march, strong, through dating.

Zac's angle
on 2nd chapter:

What had changed in dating world?

As a lady in my mid-twenties with deep roots of cultural influences in Asia, this chapter provides an interesting viewpoint regarding how the world of dating has evolved (or rather, dramatically changed). For someone as young as me, virtual dating is a norm, and this is how many people find their partners today.

However, various points made by the writer of Chapter 2 cannot be ignored either. When comparing it with traditional physical dating, it obviously does not seem ideal. At the same time, it is also worth noting that online dating allows various positives, and it may not be as bad as the writer has portrayed.

What I believe that virtual dating allows people to portray their true inner-self without having to worry about judgments made by the other party involved in the dating process. Discussion over texts or e-mails is very different from face-to-face discussion, and people often decide to hold various thoughts and comments during the latter form of communication. However, since people are usually sitting miles away during virtual dating, they feel freer to express their true self in such a situation. Moreover, finding an ideal partner can be a painful experience for some people, such as introverts or people with anxiety issues. But the experience can be made easier through virtual dating, since the dynamics of this type of dating are pretty different.

While Cynthia does seem to be a strange character, she does not deserve hate for that kind of personality. It is one aspect of virtual dating that people do not feel a need to fake their personality, since they are in complete control of their privacy.

What this means is that online dating makes the dating process easier, and more comfortable for a large number of people genuinely looking to find dating partners. So, virtual dating can be complemented with physical dating afterward to eradicate certain criticism.

Michelle's angle on 2nd chapter:

Who to believe and what to learn?

I am in my mid -thirties from Nigeria, Africa. Reading Chapter 2 about Cynthia and Betty reminded me of the similar situation I lived with my best friend. Do you remember Andre's interrogations about his initial dating contacts? Guess what: I had the same thing with my dear Sandy. My darling sweetheart friend since high school, I recall being on a phone call with Sandy (who had repeatedly proven that she sucked at relationships) telling me how she met a new man — whom she painted in all shades of bright colors — making me believe he was the "Mr. Right she had been waiting for."

Sandy went on and on talking about him, and the next thing I asked her was where they met. With the way she had painted him, I fantasized in advance a million places where they could have met. "Actually, we met on a dating site," she giggled. I was taken aback, and that made me throw in a lot of interrogative questions at her (which she hadn't really given a thought). "I'll never really know," Sandy said to me. "Until I give it a try." So, I sighed, and advised her to be careful nonetheless.

Frankly, I was not surprised when Sandy and I got to talk on this same issue during a lunch break. Only this time, it was not as intriguing as the last time we first got to talk about it. Sandy confessed to me her deep disappointment concerning the man she thought she knew all about. I hated to do the cliché "you-know-I-warned-you-against-this-but-you-wouldn't-listen" strategy, but I had to.

Believe me, I am not against dating sites, and neither do I wholly buy the idea. Over time, I just recorded a lot of memories I had regarding dating sites partly personal, and others consisting of various discussions with several women who shared with me the traps which one can easily fall into when using virtual dating sites without a deep knowledge beforehand. When I got to listen to my very good friend talk about her experience with the man on that particular dating site, I felt indignant that she had to go through everything Sandy went through because she had no prior idea of how these virtual dating sites are being run.

My purpose for writing these stories describing Internet dating, as I already mentioned earlier, is not to spite dating sites, but to properly emphasize certain rules guiding and avoiding misconceptions behind those virtual dating sites. So, this includes the simple things you wouldn't be told before embarking on a dating site, unless you have to learn it yourself, which usually does not end well if wrongly applied.

Trust me, dating sites can be fun if you know the basic rules and act accordingly. More so, this dating-sharing experiences book is an important learning tool, filled with surprising life engagements pertaining to virtual dating sites. It also consists of subtle humor and simple tactics, to help each individual in his/her soulmate search.

Andreina's angle
on the 2nd chapter:

Presenting yourself fairly is a challenge.

I am twenty-three years old from Colombia, South America. Writing about my personality on dating sites has always been a struggle for me. Like, I don't want to sound too pretentious talking too right about me, but I don't want people to believe that I'm not worthy either. Finding a real balance is hard for me.

One day, my cousin Estefania told me that the description wasn't about selling myself, but about selling the idea that I am so much more than I appear to be. And it made total sense to me, because people usually get a wrong idea of me due to my appearance. I instantly fell for the idea of writing a description that could show others that I'm not just a pretty girl.

The fact that I'm Colombian usually attracts the attention a lot of foreign guys. Even in my city (Bogota), I attract the attention of many men. They like my curves and my long hair. They always say I'm the prettiest girl they have ever seen. But, this should not influence my online presentation. However, they usually think that I'm the kind of girl that uses her body to accomplish things. The kind of girl that's stupid and empty. They think that I can only be used for sex, or that I'm the kind of woman that takes advantage of men in exchange for sex.

That I'm a prostitute. I can't even have sex with someone I don't share a bond with. I'm just not that kind of girl. It's pretty disappointing when guys just reach out to me because they think I'm a prostitute. This is why describing my personality is so important: because I don't get a chance to introduce myself in real life.

Guys just make the impression they want to make of me right after taking a single look at me. But it's different when it comes to online dating. People don't usually trust others based only on their profile pictures. They are a little more curious. They want to make sure that the person on that profile picture is real, so they read people's profiles looking to have enough information to make a proper judgment. Besides, no one wants to waste their time with someone that doesn't want the same things they do.

So, I need to express my interests. Acting is my passion. I love good training sessions at the gym and eating healthy. I value my family and friends above anything else on the planet. I'm a dog person. I enjoy cooking and baking for the people I love. I spend my Sunday's hiking. That I'm looking for the right person to share all my passions with. I want guys to know that I'm more than what they see. And if they are willing to listen to me, I would love to get to know what kind of person they are too. As you can see, describing me without sounding cheesy can be complicated. But I do my best, and so far, it has worked pretty well.

Rose Lin's angle on 2nd chapter:

The relative meaning of dating profiles.

I haven't seen any book like Andre's product. He is ardent at fashioning and pitching himself — clearly exposed — in this world of online dating. At least he is not living in China, like me.

His motto: "To me, patience is as paramount virtue, just like sense of humor. A mixture of both will give an almost perfect partner." So, I will say with my experience: anyone will kill (not meant literally) to have such a partner. And eventually, some people will come for the kill.

But, let's back to Chapter 2.

I think Cynthia is one of the many persons looking for love online, but does not know that there is not just one, but numerous forbidden fruits in the Eden of online dating. You can stay genuine in real life (sorry, traditional) dating sphere. But online, you must be at least "almost a perfect partner." Traditional dating gives you the room to grow up, but online dating is for true grown-ups.

Then there's Betty. My kind of person, I guess? She has the speed of a gazelle, but unlike her, I have learned the importance of slowing down and waiting.

The above chat records clearly reveal the demanding need to meet a perceived universal standard in online dating. But, the overriding power of what standard means remains in the hands of individuals whose profiles, ironically, aim to sell out as the standard.

I think the big question is: does the next person online find you as a product worthy of exchange?

Tania's angle on 2nd chapter:

The 'yang' side of Cynthia and Betty does exist.

Being already thirty-three years old from Lisbon, Portugal, I would like to share my take on this special book. Funny how people see the same thing in a different way. When I read Cynthia's description, I felt it to be very Yin/Yang: the balance of Tao, and the acceptance of the Tao law that says that everything that has a front has a back.

Actually, in a world where so many people live of virtual appearance, it's kind of refreshing to see someone who admits that she has both sides. She is not always the happy and joyful person. That she also has sad moments and that, for her, it is important that her soulmate will be with her in all moments.

This is actually something which is highly important to me. I can be very introverted at times, especially when I am a little more down. Whether in romance or in friendship, I'm not interested in people that are all around me when I am in my party mood, but put me aside when I'm in a more introverted mood.

Fortunately, I have a lot of friends who truly accept both my sides. To hang out with me even when I'm in an introverted mood. If I had to write what I was looking for in a man (and I actually did in the form of an intention letter some time ago), being someone who is able to share not only my happiest, highly positive and active moments, but also my introverted, melancholic ones was of highly importance. To feel good at my side in all of them is definitely a priority.

I am allowed to be sad, and I must say that sometimes I really enjoy being in a more melancholic mood. As someone who believes that we should learn how to accept and flow with all our emotions (to know how to deal with them instead of repressing them), Cynthia's description sounds to me like an honest presentation. And it's good if it scares away some people. It's probably because they are not the right men for her, and she is not the right woman for them. That is completely fine of course. A fake virtual happiness does not seduce me at all.

I do feel that you dismiss her at high speed. And Betty... well, we have a saying in Portugal: "She made the party, launched the fireworks and caught the (I don't know what the English word for that part is that fireworks would fall on earth)."

But the idea is there: she basically made the entire conversation, and got to her conclusions all by herself. I wonder about her insecurities. Somehow, she tends to think she's bothering people right away.

Clara's angle
on the 2nd chapter:

Initial try-out as an innocent lady in twenties.

My experience with online dating/virtual dating is totally different from Andre's. Like Andre, I'm not a big fan of dating sites. Yes, Cynthia and Betty's short interactions had their meaning as learning life references. Dating sites have their perks (like meeting more people in a short time and making friends along the way), even if you don't find your soulmate. I love meeting people in real life and seeing them in their true selves, without them trying to impress me or sound like what I want.

Sometimes, it might be the opposite of what I want in a man, but it can also become very attractive. Remember in the magnet theory: same sides repel and opposite sides attract. Okay, back to my experience before I go into science that I don't fully understand (laughing out loud).

My experience was on Facebook. Yes, it's not the typical dating site, but believe me, a lot of dating goes on there. We meet a lot of friends, prospective business partners and soulmates. I know tons of people (and friends) who are in serious relationships with people they met on Facebook, so I can't begin to list. But this is about my experience, not theirs (tongue out). I'm sorry, I play too much. Setting up my profile was not hectic. I just didn't know if I should remix my name like other girls were doing, because I didn't want to sound shallow-minded, presumptuous, or desperate. for example, names like:

| **Full name:** | Clara White |
| **Facebook name:** | boobilicioussandy4life |

I just can't stop laughing at this name, and believe me, I am not attacking anyone. This name was just picked randomly. So, I go with my middle name and last name.

Here my profile:

Details:	26 years old female.
Height:	5ft 4inches.
City:	Lagos, Nigeria.
Profession:	Freelance writer/ Entrepreneur.
Education:	bachelor of Science (Mass communication).
Smokes?	No.
Has children?	No.
Personality:	Open-minded.
Looking for:	Men.
For:	Serious relationship.
Race:	African.
Drinks alcohol?	Socially.
Figure:	In between slim and plump.
Animals:	Not currently, but I love dogs.
Second language:	Yoruba. "Je parle Français un peu". (Very little of French, I love it).
Does drugs?	No.
Hair:	Black.
Eye color:	Brown.
Has a car:	No.
Astrological sign:	Capricorn.
Wants kids?	Yes.
Longest relationship:	6 years.
Are you ambitious:	Yes.
Hobbies:	Movies, dancing, music, writing, drawing and cooking.
Religious views:	I believe in Christ.
Favourite quote:	Don't be afraid to try anything new, amateurs built the ark and professionals built the Titanic.

Whew! Done with that. Afterwards, I upload a full picture of me, then I take a chill pill. By chill pill, I mean relax and see how it goes. On May 15th, I receive a message on my Facebook messenger from Tim.

2:55pm May 15th Tim:

Hi Clara, I love your profile and hope we could talk more, if you want to. Tim

Upon receiving the message, I dash to his profile immediately. He was Egyptian, 5ft 8 inches. Good looks and curly hair, 30 years old, and an entrepreneur. I find his profile interesting, so I reply.

3:01 pm May 15th Clara:

Hi Tim, thanks for the message. I find your profile interesting too. Are you based in Egypt?

I ask because even though I find his profile interesting, I don't want a very long-distance relationship, so maybe just friendship. My phone buzzes with messages again, it's Tim. Yaay, I find myself very excited.

3:06pm May 15th Tim:

Hi Clara, yes, I am based in Egypt and I see you are based in Nigeria. But to me, distance is not a problem because I want something serious with you. Traveling to Nigeria is not a problem for me. Can you please send me a recent picture? Tim

I stand up to dance by shaking my booty to an imaginary song which stuns my cousin who is my flatmate (hee-hee). I am excited because he doesn't mind coming to my country just to see me. This means he is serious. I have to really get to know him before I start fantasizing, so I send him a full picture, then ask for his, which he sends. Then drops another message.

3:25pm May 15th Tim:

I must say I love your skin color, smile and body structure. I don't mean to be forward, but do you think we can be in a relationship because I am beginning to like you very much. Tim

Immediately, I am flushed by his compliments and my cavewoman instincts start to kick in, so I decide to take it slow.

3:30 May 15th Clara:

Thank you for the compliments. I like your looks too. Yes, I believe we can, but first, we need to get to know each other. What do you do for a living?

3:35 pm May 15th Tim:

Good you believe so too. I have a store for house hold items and run a family business selling tiles. What are you up to now, please send your picture.

I told I was watching a movie and sent him a picture. I found it exciting and also suspicious that he wanted various pictures, but I felt he just wanted to verify it was truly me.

3:40 May 15th Tim:

You are really a pretty African woman, with good bust and hips. Now, I want to come to Abuja, Nigeria. Will you be free next week, so I can come? I will like to spend three days with you alone. I hope it's not rude to say I am sexually attracted to you. Tim

Now I begin to feel he his desperate and is pursuing something else. But I have learnt not to jump to conclusions, so I wait.

3:45pm May 15th Clara:

Tim, don't you think it's too early to come all the way to Nigeria to see me. You don't know me well. What if I don't match what you want in a soulmate?

3:47pm May 15th Tim:

I have no doubts Clara, and I don't mind coming all the way for you baby. I will book my ticket tonight, if you want. Please, I have to go now, but please send me a picture of you, but this time with less cloth and more skin. Tim.

"What!" I yell as I read his message, making my cousin drop her cup of tea. I realize he likes me for my body. I'm not saying it's wrong to be attracted to me sexually (in fact it's very important) but asking for nude pictures is disrespectful. Also, he is not interested in my personality. Being very offended, I decide to end the chat.

3:53 May 15th Clara:

Thanks for your honesty Tim and I really like you too, but I don't think we match in terms of what I want in a man. Good luck in finding the woman of your dreams.

3:55pm May 15th Tim:

What did I say to offend you, my Clara. Please give me another chance to prove I am the man for you. I love you. Tim

I read his message but ignore it, and this time I am very irritated. He loves me? How is that possible under an hour? It is obvious he just wants sex. I ignore his message and drink a glass of water.

I play Billy Jean by Michael Jackson, and as I listen, I find the whole Tim scenario amusing. I find myself laughing. Will a man really come all the way to another country to fulfill his sexual fantasy? I guess I am not finding any soulmate today, so I drop my phone and see a movie to clear my head.

Nio's angle
on the 2nd chapter:

Love is not exclusive hetero-sexual term.

Oh, dear Andre, how admirable is your ability to describe yourself so perfectly with that sureness. I (even though I already have more than two decades over me) still have moments when I have no idea of what I am or what I want. But for you, I've made up my way to this daring approaching. Very similar to the one I've used (casually) on the online dating site like Omegle, here's my personal profile:

Name: Niobe, Mariana but friends call me Nio.

Age: 25 y/o from Caracas in Venezuela.

Status: Trying my best to get my degree, I've been the last 2 years convincing myself to complete my thesis, of a beautiful career called: "Bachelor of Audiovisual Arts". I married the arts and I haven't married a person, although I have a suitor, of my age, which until now seems to be "the one", and we've been living in concubinage for a while.

How hard is it to recognize the true love! Isn't it? Just like it happened to you (and so many others), I've gone through a variety of "mistakes." I'm sorry, I'll correct: "learnings," because just as you said, each experience leaves a mark on us and makes us stronger.

And, in the end, the search of love is a search of identity as well, don't you think? To know with certainty what is what we want it is necessary to discover exactly what we are made of.

One of the identity conflicts I had to deal with was my sexual preferences. Since I was young, I've felt attracted to the opposite sex as much as my own. When you are young, you have no idea of the possibility of being bisexual. As a result, I discarded: "Since I like men, I'm not gay".

So, I decided I was hetero, and started going for the conquest of those young men I liked. I had what I thought was a "pretty clear" idea of my aspirations. The ideal man for me should be:

- Handsome
- Smart
- Funny
- Honest (and faithful)
- Affectionate

But having my goals clear didn't help me at all. I had the bad luck to fall in love with guys who already had a girlfriend, or with my best friends (who never felt the same for me). For several years, I became a sad example of what "friendzone" means.

I got to the college, and I made friends with Carla — a really open-minded girl. As it happened with men, after a while being friends, I started thinking I was in love with her. In a rare necessity of trying the forbidden fruit, I had my first kiss with her, and after that (although I enjoyed it), I realized that what I was feeling for her was not true love, but rather a relentless curiosity.

Carla made me think I was a lesbian, and that I had to change my searching area of true love to the female gender side. That's how I started sailing on the dangerous ship of the online dating sites. I made my first homosexual profile, and the hunting started. My aspirations were now a little more mature (or so I thought). My ideal woman should be:

- Of thin build, regardless of ethnic origin or skin color.
- Intelligent enough to exchange thoughts and preferences.
- Honest, regardless of strict fidelity, as long as both parties agree.

- Should have a good sense of humor - since I am an irremediable joker.
- Should be affectionate, regardless of whether it tends towards the more feminine or more masculine appearance.
- Should have life goals.

After plenty of shipwrecks, I found Amanda on one of the online sites. Amanda was a pretty accurate approach to love. We had a nice relationship that lasted more than two years, and ended when she obtained a scholarship to a Spain university, having to leave the country. Yet, the breaking didn't break me, and it served for me to realize that it was not love either.

Life goes around and comes around, and one of the dates I had after the rupture presented her best friend to me: Ender. a pretty funny guy with photographer aspirations. Until then I THOUGHT I had my mind clear, but here it was where love arrived and drove over me like a heavy truck. It was so fast I couldn't even see it coming.

Ender hypnotized me practically immediately. I totally forgot about my pretended homosexuality, and about all the specific requirements anybody should have to be my partner. I was just feeling that I wanted to be next to him the full twenty-four hours a day, the seven days a week, and that was enough for me to say "Yes!" when he asked me to be his girlfriend, just two weeks after we met.

We've known each other better since then. I realized (thank goodness) that he effectively applies to all the boyfriend requirements I had. With him, I learned that bisexuality is real, and that's exactly how I define myself now to family and acquaintances. As was expected, they insist that I'm really hetero, that I am passing through a "phase."

It doesn't matter. One should not let others affect you for what you say or think. what really matters is feeling good about yourself. So, they can say anything they want, but I found what I wanted: a serious relationship.

Morgan's angle
on the 2nd Chapter:

Be cautious when posting your profile.

Despite being in my early twenties, I had several years of online dating experiences. My nickname is Morgan. I am a young writer, was born in Turkey, and I am living today in Dubai, UAE. Our generation is born with online communications, including various opportunities such as dating or finding love online. While there are many benefits to it, it also comes along with a few disadvantages. Andre asked me to share my part of learned lessons, which I am glad to do.

First and foremost, be cautious about what you share with others. Keep your profile low-key. You do not want an unknown stranger to stalk you. Try to be as conservative as you can be. Do not release private information like your location, card number, or places you go publicly. Finding someone good online can be quite difficult, particularly if you have a lot of expectations. But do not lose hope. Communicate and meet as many people you want. If you do not like someone, tell them and proceed onward with your search.

Social sites like Facebook, Instagram and Snapchat are some of the most popular sites for young people to find someone. Be within your circle, look for what you want, and do not just time pass with random strangers because you feel lonely. If you like someone, straightforwardly tell them! Do not wait for the right opportunity, because we all know that it never comes. Try not to be tricked by looks. You probably think that he's attractive and he has six pack abs, so he is the perfect man for me. Looks are deceiving! Some people turn out to be the complete opposite of what they look like while some people may be beautiful on the inside as well as the outside.

One of the drawbacks of online dating is catfishes; they are every-where, on every site, with different details and pictures. They are identified as young women and men, with seducing pictures. It can be difficult to spot out a catfish, but simply ask them for a picture of themselves to prove it they are real or not. If they hesitate, then chances are they are using someone else's identity as theirs.

Do not share explicit photos with anyone. Many individuals in dating sites are usually found asking for nudes or explicit photos. If someone asks you, kindly turn them down. You do not want to be exposed, particularly if it's somebody you haven't met! These photographs can circulate around the web, and that may show a bad image of you. Keep yourself private until you have found someone trustworthy.

Now let's get onto the good part of online dating: How you can successfully find someone nice who matches to your desires. Communication is the key! Once you have matched with a decent person, the best thing you can do is learn about them; communicate with them, ask them how their day/night was, ask what worst thing they is have done in their life, ask how much sarcasm they take, what plans they have for future, etc. Joke around while chatting so you even learn about their sense of humor. Nobody wants anyone who is extra serious with fury rubbed in his face.

Learn about their hobbies, weaknesses and strengths. See whether they are good at controlling anger or not. Once you have done all this, make a move to meet them. Visit them or their country. Naturally, a human will bond with you if they like you, and if they do, then that's stunning. But do not stop there. Keep your online communication constant; learning new things about your partner never hurts.

Share your real pictures online, do not fake yourself, and do not fake your personality or looks. You wouldn't want that to happen to you, right?

Explore and grab all the opportunities given in these free online dating sites and apps. You have nothing to lose! Online dating can get very surprising at some points. You may find someone completely different from what you expected, or you may find someone who reaches your expectations. With online dating, a long-distance relationship comes, and this is when individuals find it difficult to keep it. If your partner is interested in you, then he/she will have no issue with being in a long-distance relationship. It isn't that difficult.

Loyalty and a strong connection helps.

If you are young, and looking for relationships/love, go ahead. Many teenagers have access to social sites and dating apps; although their age limit is 18, you can still try in free social apps. Be mature in taking decisions and meeting people; you do not want to be tied with the wrong person. If you are meeting someone completely new, I would suggest meeting in a public place with a friend. This way you will not be harmed.

Lastly, consider dating a couple of individuals before settling down with someone in a relationship. Do not jump right into dates or going out. Baby steps; learn about them. If your expectation matches, then go. Otherwise, continue with your journey to find the right man.

Online dating is like investigating a murder case: you are the detective, and you find clues in different people. You learn new things about different people, and in the end, you finally catch the murderer.

And he is just what you were looking for!

You don't want to fall in love with a murderer though…

CHAPTER 3

Always Read the Profile
Before Answering

April 7th – 3:37 p.m. Lilly1920 wrote:

Hello Mr. Charming!

I offer you this flower in homage to your profile that has been able to draw my attention and encourage me to write to you.

Your writings are invigorating, and I am interested in knowing a little more about you!

I am looking for a life partner with whom to share the great and small projects that will come to mind.

And what a beautiful moment, in this marvellous sunny day of the end of winter, to discover this unusual man, and to whom I could make discover all the charming little attentions capable of raising all the pleasures.

In fact, seriously speaking, I am looking for a long-term relationship, and I dare to believe that there is a person with whom it will be possible to build wonderful memories that will embellish our minds.

So, if you are interested in making contact to discover our affinities, I will be happy to answer you.

Looking forward to reading from you,

Isabel

Finally, a charming soul that is not afraid to express herself freely with qualities worthy of a potential book writer. I ask myself the question (legitimate, in my opinion): To how many men has she sent this message, almost too perfect to be spontaneous? Is she my match? Is she as beautiful as her writing?

Sometimes you must take risks in life and believe. You never know. She may perhaps be this rare pearl I'm looking for.

I go back to her profile to find some additional information. She is five feet five inches tall, the minimum limit for my six feet two inches. This is a limit I set for myself—quite arbitrarily, I admit—but to which I hold. The only photo in her profile is a bit blurred. It shows a cute and swarthy face, but I cannot see her features clearly.

I am not ashamed to say or write it: For me, physical appearance is an important criterion of attraction. The natural human desire must be present in order for me to even consider any romantic relations at all. But goodness me—am I not seeking my soulmate?

I answer Lilly1920 after long reflection—too long, perhaps, for a mature man because my answer is quite short.

April 7 – 5:12 p.m. Vivaldi17 writes:

Hello Isabel,

Thank you very much for this lovely introduction. What attracted you to reading my profile?

Thank you

Andre

While waiting for a reply from Lilly1920, I look attentively to a second message, this one from a certain Airelle007.

It is important not to waste your time in this new, virtual world of dating. Everything is instantaneous and everything, it seems, is to be consumed on the spot. In the name of progress, then, I adapt my behavior to the times because a failure to respond immediately may signal a lack of interest and result in a lost opportunity. But, of course, the question remains: Is this indeed a real opportunity?

April 7 – 3:39 p.m. Airelle007 writes:

Hello Vivaldi17,

I'm sending you a first message to get in touch with you.
I find your profile Interesting. Later, Zoe.

I am beginning to enjoy this. It took time to write my profile, yet what I've written seems to be working. After all, I am in conversation with two women simultaneously! I feel like a teenager, but I must not lose perspective.

"Being" in virtual space is like playing with soulless objects. The true nature – the human dimension – behind all such profiles, including my own, remains to discovered. The dangers inherent in that initial uncertainty explains why so many women must present themselves anonymously on online dating sites. I get it and, my feet once again on firm ground, I respond:

April 7 – 5:17 p.m. Vivaldi17 wrote:

Thanks, Zoe.

What turns you on in my profile?

Andre

April 7 – 5:27 p.m. Airelle007 wrote:

I like the fact that you mention that you're emotionally stable and that you're indulgent.

You seem like a balanced man and feel good.

I also hung on the phrase that says that you love cooking.

You seem to be well cultured and interesting.

In addition, I find your face attractive. :-)

I think that's a lot of positive points, isn't it?

And what does my profile tell you about me?

Zoe.

An excellent response. From her profile on POF, she seems lovely. A beautiful Asian face with the aura of a mature woman. She looks younger than her years. I am rapidly being seduced, or should I say wooed?

Then, as I read on, a problem. Oh, no! She measures only five feet one inch (155 cm) in height. My true caveman prejudice takes the upper hand. I really should have looked at her profile before replying immediately. Cirque du Soleil acrobatics are not my thing. I fear I must beat a hasty retreat, without offending this charming person.

April 7th– 5:33 p.m. Vivaldi17 wrote:

Hello Zoe.

This site is a showcase. As you know, behind our profiles hide real people.

I just looked at your profile, and I see a big physical challenge in height (not wanting to play with words). We have more than one foot of difference.

What do you think?

Her reply does not take long.

As I open her message, I am hoping she'll understand the impossibility of the thing between us. One foot is like Mount Everest to me. I like to see eye-to-eye—or at least close to it—and not be looking so far downhill. I do not wish to risk a sprained back, a torticollis, or lumbago. After passing a certainage, one must pay attention to one's back.

But when I read her response I find, alas, that she just doesn't get it.

April 7th– 5:47 p.m. Airelle007 wrote:

I understand it's a lot, but I am pretty and I know how to wear high heels.

As told by a friend, "What you seek will always find you if you persist," which I keep repeating to myself since

I registered on this site. It is not an obvious thing to showcase, but in the society in which we live, meeting meaningful people is a challenge.

Lamartine wrote: "One person misses you and life is a desert."

I have friends and a family but would like to share my life with a man who wants to get involved and share beautiful moments. I think it's smarter to do things together. Like everyone else, I love cinema. The last film I watched was "The Golden Lady."

I liked it. I love watching shows (what I regularly do). I appreciate humorous shows than those of popular or classical music. I love almost all musical genres. In short, I'm quite versatile in my tastes. The world is wide and travelling attracts me. France remains my favourite destination! Good food and good wine: yum!

Zoe

I re-read her response many times, trying to find clues on how to elegantly terminate this conversation. But it is difficult. I find no obvious flaws in her presentation or in her response.

The difficulty may, of course, be with me. I know myself, and I am uncomfortable with the radical difference in height. I ask myself if I'm not the one who has become, over time, too old for these dating games. Who knows?

In the end, the only way out may be to feign lack of interest, which is really untrue. I send her a cut-and-paste of my previous answer to Lessens69.

April 7th – 6:17 pm Vivaldi17 wrote:

Thank you, Zoe, for your message. I visited your profile. As you know, the goal of an approach on this site is to recognize a mutual physical attraction. However, I don't think it's the case. For me at least.

Sincerely, Andre.

Obvious lesson learned: Remember to look, in detail, at the profile of the person writing before answering emails!

I'm sure there is more to be learned from my brief exchange with Zoe, but I've been all of five hours on this site and there are already five more messages awaiting. My confidence returns. That's a very good average per hour. Long live the Internet!

Of the five, there are three I'd rather forget, one to discover, and one to answer later.

But Isabel (Lilly1920) is not among the lot. Has Isabel—she of the blurred, olive-skinned features I cannot place in Africa, Asia or beyond—had second thoughts? I am quite anxious to know.

The Internet shrinks our planet, bringing distant souls together, and in so doing exponentially enlarges our dating possibilities. Is it for the best? I think so. The only block to meeting people of every sort is our own spirit and capacity to remain open-minded.

But now, because I haven't heard back from Isabel, my mind races, her well-crafted words echoing in my head. I hear the strains of Carlos Santana's classic, "Black Magic Woman," bubbling up in my mind, but the lyrics, this time, are my own:

> I'm turning my back, honey.
> Speaking of back, I am paying attention to mine.
> So, despite your promises of happiness,
> Your boundless kindness,
> Your infinite depth of soul,
> And your high heels,
> I pass over my stupidity to another call!

And therein lies the danger.

Another lesson learned: It may not be online dating we need to fear but, rather, the often ridiculous mental and emotional acrobatics we indulge in as we pursue it! I think it may be time to get off the slippery slope of virtual exchanges and onto the solid ground of real-life, real-time encounters. But before plunging into that abyss, I have the feeling I had better have a plan.

Debrillyn's angle
on the 3rd chapter:

Road map for meaningful date.

Online dating for a young lady like me in her 20s from Texas, USA has been an instrumental tool for meeting a lot of people and expanding my dating pool. However, we need to be careful because a few people send awkward messages that are sometimes disrespectful. The profile is very important, as it gives you an insight about the person. But, even if the person matches your ideal profile in terms of height, physique, likes, hobbies and others, then chemistry and compatibility cannot be guaranteed.

I have been on a few dates with men I met online. But for me, the biggest thing is to preserve your patience. Meeting someone online for the first time and having a short conversation allows you to see if there is palpable chemistry and flow, otherwise it instantly kills off any hope of going out. I can assure you: I can get a feel for the person through chatting over several days or weeks to discern characteristics of an ideal partner or not. Expressed attitude is like visible smoke, so it is difficult to hide. If a person is a jerk, or someone without morals, it would not be hard to spot over time.

Online dating (although virtual) is very similar to in person dating. Feelings have to be developed, and it has to be mutual for it to stand a chance. Sometimes, you just see a person's profile picture and you instantly get that feeling. But if the person doesn't connect back, it is better to just let go.

The next step for me after developing a form of friendship through the online platform is to meet the person physically. Most times, I choose something light for a first date. We could just grab a cup of coffee and enjoy each other's company. Most times, it is easier for me to enjoy such dates because we must have had so much fun together online before getting to this point. The twist here is occasionally, people can be entirely different to what you imagine while chatting with them online.

If I am turned off at this point, nothing would materialise any further from the date.

Virtual dating works and I am proud to say I have met a few dream dates online. Online dating has evolved over time and is not the same today as it was before. It is now a multi-billion-dollar industry. A significant percentage of American couples met online, and I am currently in a serious relationship with someone I met online.

The demerit is that a lot of people pretend to be someone else, which not always meets the reality. Profile pictures and other details about a person can be totally misleading. It's important to be cautious of how you deal with people you meet through online dating.

Usually, engaging in video calls and taking a lot of time before meeting the person is always helpful. Being true to myself when dealing with a date online is also a key paramount, because it helps me to know if the other party admires me or just likes me as a person.

Clara's angle on the 3rd chapter:

Read profile carefully, line by line.

I'm currently trying to get over my first mishap about my profile on online dating sites, while working on my laptop and taking my early morning cup of coffee. Believe me, I can't do without my black coffee. It's like fuel to my engine. Alright, back to my computer. While I admire my cup of coffee, a message pops up on my screen: Facebook Messenger. I dump my coffee and delve online, like a dog chasing a bone (not that dramatic though).

8:00am May 16th John writes:

Hi Clara, I find your profile very interesting, especially seeing that we both share some similarities in views. I would like to talk to you more.

I noticed he had sent it by 8 am, and it was 9 am already. And from the picture, I can see he is very, not to say extremely, cute. Do I go ahead to read his profile now? I see we are birthday mates, but I can't finish because the time is ticking in my head. Oh my God, what if he thinks I don't like him, so I reply.

9:01am May 16th I write:

Hi John, sorry for the delayed reply. I just turned on my computer. Oh, I see we are birthday mates. So, what other things are you interested in?

While I await his reply, I go through his profile, but pictures first. Soon, I find myself in Hawaii with John. He's a bundle of hotness. To think he can become my personal hot chocolate. He's dark-skinned, broad chest, 5ft 8 inches, and his smile is to kill for. I stare especially at the picture where he is shirtless and I find myself day dreaming of me being in those hands. I notice he had replied, so I quickly go through the rest of his profile and that's where I fall hard on my buttocks. He's an ATHEIST. "Noooooooooooooooooooo!"

9:05am May 16th John writes:

Hi, Clara. Thank you for replying. I was beginning to think you didn't like me. I find the fact that you're an artist in your way very attractive, and I feel we just might be soulmates. So, what do you like about me?

I loved everything about him, but his belief is a turn off for me. So, I decide to be honest with him. I just hope he won't take it the wrong way or feel offended.

9:10am May 16th I write:

Hi, John. Sincerely, I like everything about your profile especially your pictures, oh my. But we share different beliefs. I am a Christian and you are an Atheist. Believe me, I respect your beliefs, but I don't think we can be soulmates. Thanks for messaging me.

I lick my wounds again. I guess I should have read his profile first before replying. Now, I feel very silly. Anyway, I hope for more hot chocolates in the future.

Helen's angle
on the 3rd chapter:

Always read the profile is a reminder.

Being in my early thirties from Alaska as tech- savvy generation, there are many reasons why a person would choose to date online rather (or in addition to) dating in a person-to-person encounter. After all, online dating is based on your own life schedule, and can be as personal or impersonal as you would like it to be.

Dating online can be a great way to get to know someone without having to reveal too much of yourself at once. With the privacy the internet affords, you can keep certain personal details to yourself until you feel more comfortable, or until you feel you've gotten to know someone better. It's important to keep in mind that not everyone on a dating website is genuine.

Approach online dating with an air of caution; make sure not to reveal any details about your location or other information that would make it easy for someone to find you. Even if you've chosen someone to get to know better, let the process take its time and gradually reveal information one piece at a time.

In my past experience on dating sites, I never really had time to read through people's profiles. I preferred to see their pictures and make assumptions from them. This was not a good idea, as I learned in the following exchange:

April 15, 14:25, Frank wrote:

Hi, how are you doing?

Without reading his profile, I made an instant reply.

April 15, 14:26; Helen

Hello Frank, Thanks for viewing my profile and finding some interest. Can we get to know each other?

April 15, 14:27; Frank

Thanks for your reply Helen. I am the shy type and I don't usually know how to start a conversation, especially with ladies. I am an Entrepreneur who works as a Freelance with several industries and at height 7'2" who loves to be romantic with the woman of my dreams, and I think we will get along very well since you are also a freelancer.

I realized I had to put an INSTANT END to the chat so as not to waste more time. I don't like my man at that ridiculous height. 7'2"?! Not for me. Thanks. And I cannot date a Freelancer because I am, too, and I know it will be very bad.

April 15, 14:30; Helen

Thanks for this brief introduction. Actually, you have amazing personality. But I cannot build my relationship on Freelancing concept. It will be such a disaster to even consider. Thanks for showing an interest in me, it was a great chatting experience.

So, I've learned that it's best read the profile first!

Kata's angle
on the 3rd chapter:

What matter most, our size or the truth?

First, I would like to present myself as a Hungarian lady in my early 20's (coming from Budapest in the European) who experienced extensive travel and living abroad. Had I read this a few years back, I would have rolled my eyes – because really, you like someone based on everything but their height? How shallow can you be?

But I've been in the same shoes. I'm a whopping 160 cm short, so when I was living in certain places on this beautiful and grand planet of ours, even most women seemed to tower over me. I'd imagine how tiny I was compared to men. Yeah, shorty running after Mr Daddy-Long legs as he casually strolls down the street.

However, height isn't always the only thing that should be regarded carefully. At least in public that can be corrected (heels are a woman's best friend, after all). And well, bedroom stuff can be managed for sure. But sometimes, you might come into obstacles you would not even expect– and merely because you are too lazy to ride the couple lines people use to charmingly describe themselves. I've noticed something most of us like to brag about: skills. And that can be great when it comes down to it. I'm not even talking about the sex-stuff.

It would be best to be able to at least talk to the people you decide to go out with, right? Well, trust me; I've had instances when even that was not possible. At some point, I've lived in countries where I did not speak the local language well enough. I would get a whole ton of messages coming from guys that were (safe to say) smoking' hot, but did not speak a word of English. Now, I was quick to understand their profiles because I could get by when it came to skimming through text, but writing? It was h-e-l-l, or at least, something close to that. Being the innocent twenty-something year old that used to believe that everyone speaks English, well…

Trust me, trying to date online was a true eye-opener. And here is when useful bragging comes in. Since English, apparently, was not such a widely-spoken language in some places, people adored putting the little flag on their profiles (or even write it out) to showcase that they could be trusted. Well, mostly.

Some were dodgy of course, but it was a great filter. Of course, this is a rather personal issue (not everyone lives abroad) but it definitely proves that it's best to read everything when it comes to introductions. Sometimes, it can be very obvious while you like someone based on how they look or the first two lines of their profiles. But really, you might not like them because of something else.

It's annoying to get somewhat worked up about talking to someone, only to realize that you won't be able to talk to them other than chanting off food-names. It's a lot easier if you are attentive: after all, if people are saying the truth about themselves, at least you save yourself a few minutes (or, end up chatting up people that think that if you go out with them you'll be there free English teacher. Go figure.).

Andreina's angle on the 3rd chapter:

Online expectations and the reality.

As an early 20's old woman from Bogota, I have to admit that Andre's answer to Zoe surprised me. Not because of what he said, but because of his intentions. From my experience, if guys lose interest in you, they just stop talking to you. They don't usually explain why or try not to hurt your feelings, they literally disappear. The ones who at least give you an answer is to say something like "I made a mistake with you. Bye." And that's it. So, I think that Andre was not only honest, but also thoughtful, and I liked that.

Finding nice guys on the internet is very hard these days. It's like 80% of them are after one thing, if you know what I mean.

Dating apps aren't exactly for finding a romantic partner, are they? But at first glance, I find this exchange between Andre and Zoe very romantic. Am I the only one who sees it that way? It's like they're genuinely interested in each other's personality and lives in their initial exchanges. This is what I usually look for; to have a real connection with someone, getting to know them a little bit more. But that has been really hard to get.

I'm not saying that all of my experiences on online dating have been bad; I have had pretty good ones. The remarkable ones were with an Italian guy and a Canadian guy. They both were sweet and kind, and I get the feeling that Andre could be that kind of person.

Being a Latin girl makes it easy for me to find boys to have a nice chat with, because for some reason, everybody thinks that all of us look like Jennifer López or Sofía Vergara. Although there are a lot of women like them on this side of the globe, there are many kinds of beauty. However, as soon as guys know you're Latina, you immediately get all of their attention. Which I'm not going to lie, can be very nice and exciting.

Talking about this makes me want to go online for a while to see if I can find someone like Andre to talk to. I mean, I speak Spanish (the sexiest language, apparently), I know how to dance salsa and merengue, and I fit his height expectations... what could possibly go wrong?

Anyhow, dating online has always been something exciting for me. A picture or a profile description isn't enough when what you want is to find a soulmate. You have to blindly trust the other person; trust your instincts and fall for the person you think they are. And I feel like that's the opposite of everything this society has tried to teach us. Not everything has to be physical to be real; Andre and Zoe know it very well, as I do too. But to realize that — to get there — one must be brave and be open to new experiences and feelings. This is, in a way, a game. You have to rely on your instincts, think fast, engage others using just words, and hope for the best.

Tania's angle
on the 3rd chapter:

Can we read profile and guess a soulmate?

Following line of thought, regarding Lilly's message in Chapter 3, I again felt in a contrary way to you. It just seems so rehearsed that it sounds unnatural. It's beautiful yes, but people don't talk to each other like that, and that is certainly not her way when face-to-face. I always feel very distrustful when someone online speaks with such rehearsed text.

Regarding Arielle, I must say it's very normal that she didn't get your perceived problem with the height difference. Let's face it: you were not elucidative regarding that, you asked what she thought about the height difference and she answered. Clearly for her, it was not a problem, as it is not a problem to many people. I think I wouldn't date a man that is much smaller than me, so I understand your side Andre, regarding respective heights.

Well in the end, I think you learned a good lesson. When we are face-to-face with people, we have an entire physical dialogue to assess, as well as the conversation. Online, you only have that profile. Get what you can from it, but is that enough to draw a valid conclusion about a person?

Now something of deep reflection: the possibilities of the virtual world. Are they for the best? Good question. I don't have a definitive answer. The ability of meeting people from the entire world online clearly brings amazing things and could lead for a dating purpose.

I am in several Facebook groups that put me in contact with people who share my interests, including fantasy literature, art, illustration... I get a lot from those groups, and I love to be part of them. It's a more detached connection. But my focus is not on meeting people personally, but to talk about shared interests.

I think my generation is divided into two groups: one that is emotionally dependent on social networks, and the other (much smaller one, I think) that, seeing all the crap, falsehood and sensationalism that exists online, moves in another direction. I'm definitely in the second group, and although I enjoy some of the good things the Internet brings, I prefer to keep my personal life out of the Internet.

Katia's angle on the 3rd chapter:

My profile creation and the first try-out.

During a party, my friend told me that several of our IT people at university created a dating app for our campus. They probably got together with our psychology people, but it was worth a try. I downloaded the app, created my profile, and then completely forgot about it until 2 weeks later, when I got a ding on my phone and saw: "You have a new message."

As I completely forgot about the app, I was shocked that something appeared. It was just a simple hello, and after an hour of debate whether to reply at all, I did. After an hour of interesting chit-chat, I became somewhat interested in the guy. While we may not have had many things in common, I was still enjoying the talk. That's not common with me. We sent messages back and forth for a few months, and I was still not annoyed at our everyday talks. However, as it always happens, life gets too busy and I totally ignored him. Me being me, I forgot the app, as well as him, until five months later when I receive another message from him. It did take me by surprise, but we did continue our talks, and after a few weeks, we agreed to meet for the first time.

Now comes the main part of the story, or at least the main part of the main story. You'd think that you know the person with whom you've been chatting with for four months. The date went well. We had fun, or at least I had fun as it was long since I've gone on a date. We spent the whole day exploring the city I study in. The evening was also spent nicely, with a nice dinner and ambience in the restaurant.

However, the evening didn't come to the end until we had a "fun talk" where we agreed (or better said I agreed) that we don't have a relationship. We agreed that we are just seeing each other until we see whether this "seeing-each-other" will lead us. Let's be honest here: how many of you all love this talk? I'm a big fan, as usually it goes like this:

Me: "So, how does this work now?"

A Guy: "Well, I like you, and I would like to continue this."

Me: "What's 'this'?"

A Guy: "I don't want to have a serious relationship right now, but I do want to continue seeing you."

Me: "Sure, but I'm not having sex with you."

A Guy: "Yeah, I understand and agree with you."

Me: "Awesome!"

A few days later, after a movie and cuddling in bed, the conversation goes like this:

A Guy: "Um, maybe we can go like…"

Me: "Huh? But we agreed that we wouldn't go any further."

A Guy: "Yeah, but…"

Me: "But?"

I don't think it's possible to continue the conversation that is followed by me opening the door and waiting for the guy to get out of the house. But returning to the original story, the talk once again went according to the template that has been walked through for a few years. However, the fun part came in 2 weeks, right after his birthday. I got the creepiest message ever, which ended the non-excited relationship in the best manner ever. Usually it's me who ends the relationship, but this time the message was hilarious, and I just couldn't not have fun re-reading.

Stephanie's angle on the 3rd chapter:

Being someone else on the dating site.

Reading about the experiences Andre has had with POF (Plenty of Fish) is entertaining, as well as unexpected. It's clear to see that he's bringing a great deal to a relationship, and has great insights, humor and a desire to be happy in a committed relationship. What more would these women want? And yet, when they first meet him, they seem incapable of being on their best behaviour for even a little while.

Living today as a lady in her mid-thirties in the Netherlands (half an hour drive from Amsterdam), I can say, because of my profession, I am a full-time globe trotter. The online dating business is also a planetary challenge. I believe the greatest danger in dating online is deception. It's as though people have a blank slate to rewrite their lives on. But they are not that person they portray themselves to be, and this will appear sooner or later.

So here I was, one of the few people that had never tried online dating. In Italy, I had actually set up a dating profile for a close friend who had just divorced. I had done a compelling job of portraying her, as she was swamped with replies. I also selected her photos to present her properly.

She's a fantastic girl. Although she had met her ex-husband on a dating site and had been happily married to him for five years, she decided after several weeks of texting not to meet up with any of them. Some of them appeared to be great possible matches for her. I didn't question her decision.

In this brief hiatus I had after leaving my relationship, I wondered (after seeing my friend's experience): Could it be that so many wonderful potential partners could be on these sites, just waiting for me to discover them? I wanted to know if this was an amazing source of possibilities that warranted exploration. Could it be that someone I couldn't find in my work or personal life could be found in this huge array of men that I would be matched with, solely based on my preferences?

It was a cultural journey that I felt I needed to experience, if only to know it was real.

Andre's integrity and passionate search for the right woman is a wonderful quest. It's unfortunate that thus far he's had such strange experiences with women who are not what they appear to be.

Jane's angle on the 3rd chapter:

Beginning of online dating addiction?

What an amazing chatting recollection with dating encounters, even by my South African dating standards. My name is Jane, and I am thirty-one years old from Johannesburg. So why not to share my experience regarding virtual dating and the lessons I've learned?

They say your best friend (instead of bailing you out of jail) would be there beside you. I guess that was what Lisa, my dear confident mate, intended when she signed me up on a dating site. I inevitably agreed, with her only justification being that she could not go out at night with weirdos if I wasn't doing the same.

I groaned, protested, and rolled my eyes, but she prevailed because I was bored, single, and looking for an excuse to show off my newly lost five pounds. I'd never dated blindly before. In fact, I had always been a predictable dater. My last relationship lasted four years, and we met in college. Before that, I dated my high school sweet heart until we graduated. I had no idea what I was getting into, but I felt an undercurrent of excitement at the possibilities. Could it be that "The One," the elusive One could be waiting for me on an internet page?

The first guy I went out with wasn't because of his supposed age (thirty on his profile, but his laugh lines said at least five years older) or because his interests matched mine. Lisa signed me up for the date, and practically bundled me off into the cab.

We met at a nice family restaurant: a comfortable, laid-back, non-romantic place. At first sight, I almost laughed. He was a foot shorter than it said in his profile, and a great deal older. We had a nice dinner notwithstanding; he was nice and polite. The food was delicious, and it rescued us when the conversation fell flat within the first hour. As first dates go, it wasn't bad, but it wasn't good either.

Afterward, I found myself going back to that site, and it became an addiction. Years have passed, and nothing could dissuade me from gambling with my chances, not even when I struck out in succession. I met a "struggling artist" who claimed to play in an underground band and tried to invite me to something that sounded suspiciously like an orgy party.

Afterward, I met a nice-looking great conversationalist who pulled the age old "I have to go to the bathroom" trick, then bailed and left me with the bill. So, to recap, I met men who lied about their age, weight, marital status, and even sexuality. It was like I couldn't find the one; the needle within the haystack.

Lisa finally settled with a friend from work who'd been asking her out for years, but I was stuck on my bender, chasing the thrill; the chance of a maybe. It's been two years since I went on my last online date. I did not stop because I found someone, but because I realized I'd met some good men who could have been the one, but I was too busy chasing perfection in my head that I missed it.

Iga's angle
on the 3rd chapter:

Good message in the profile always paid-out.

Hello, my name is Iga. I'm from Płock, Poland, and I'm 26 years old. I've always been the kind of person that stands in the back of a crowd, hides behind people, and doesn't want to be noticed.

Before I started online dating, I always hated the fact that men judge women by their looks. I only wanted to have a nice conversation with a male about my interests. Instead of that, I received compliments about my appearance without any deeper meaning. That's why I decided to meet someone online, and it worked! I was reluctant in the beginning, but eventually, I found it in my heart to do it. I looked up a dating site and posted a picture of me with no make-up, looking sick with dark circles under my eyes, and overall unattractive. This was supposed to scare away all of the men that were interested only in my appearance and hoped for a one-time adventure.

Fortunately for me, the first guy read my profile carefully, and was interested in my message. Not for my look. So, we connected, and he turned out to be friendly and genuinely interested! We were talking day and night about everything. Our problems, our dreams… basically about what matters the most, without any focus on the looks whatsoever. I finally felt that someone really wants to get to know me! Eventually, we met. It was a really magical moment for me. I was excited for it because I felt that I wasn't going to meet a stranger, but rather a person that I already knew exceptionally well and feel comfortable with.

After that, everything started to develop quickly. We formed a relationship and met a couple days a week, since he was living outside the town. We've been together for 7 years, but then he left the country and we started to learn to live apart. Our feelings began to fade. We gradually spoke less and less, until it got to the point of no return. So, we split up.

However, thanks to online dating, I experienced an amazing 7 years that I will never forget. First, it gave me a chance to meet a nice and caring person who was focused on talking and listening to me, not looking at me. Second — and most importantly — I got rid of the prejudice that sincere men don't really exist. Would I do it again? Definitely yes!

I realise that some women might be afraid or too shy to date online. In my opinion, there's no better solution to meeting someone online while you're shy! Think about it. You first get to know someone, and then while you actually meet in person, you don't feel uncomfortable anymore because you already know each other! Isn't it convenient? On the other hand, it has a potential risk of meeting a delusional person, but doesn't real life have this risk as well? I think it is worth trying.

Well… at least in my case it was. My story with online dating has a HAPPY ENDING, despite the fact we broke up.

CHAPTER 4

The Caveman/Cavewoman Test

In anticipation of meeting potential romantic partners in person, I devised a course of action. Why? Because, you see, I feel the need to have a plan for dealing with our baser instincts when the only previous contact has been through online exchanges. The caveman or cavewoman within always emerges, sooner or later, so how can we show our true selves without alienating or offending each other?

In an effort to aid in better understanding the complex interactions between men and women—and because I have learned not to take myself (or online dating!) too seriously—I offer for your consideration the "caveman/cavewoman test." The test provides a basis for evaluating somebody's physical reaction to a potential partner. I freely admit that it is hardly scientific, but it's fun.

In Theory

The caveman/cavewoman test taps into our reptilian brain; to be more specific, our instinctual drive to reproduce. The reptilian, or primal, brain is in charge of the four Fs: feeding, fighting, fleeing, and…well, reproduction (no profanity, please). So, when it comes to this test, forget about rational thought.

In Practice

The test is uncomplicated, but men, especially, must be very careful when administering it, lest they get slapped in the face or hauled into court. Your timing must be excellent because if you move too soon, you will get NO as an answer, and if you move too late, you may find yourself in the dreaded "friend zone." The key element to keep in mind is to strike the right balance and to have self-confidence.

Three prerequisites to a successful test:

1. You must perceive (understanding, of course, that perception may not be reality) that the test subject is interested in you. This is a minimum condition for a successful test;
2. You must believe that the person is not only interested in you, but is attracted to you as well, and that you've made a connection. This is an intermediate condition for a successful test; and
3. You share mutual respect and trust. This is the ultimate condition suitable for a successful test.

NOTE: Do not proceed unless at least one prerequisite has been met, and I would humbly suggest at least two prerequisites should be confirmed, if you are hesitant!

The Test

Move closer to the person, smile your warmest, most genuine smile, and offer them a gentle hug in your arms. That's it!

[I bet you thought something much more drastic was afoot. That's your mind at work, not my own.] The sooner you know the result of the test, the better you will feel about the person.

Genuine hugs cannot be likened to inept sexual action with bad intent, especially if undertaken with complete respect towards the dating partner.

Analysis of the Results

An accurate analysis of the results is important. Avoid hasty generalizations but trust your head and your body. You don't want a dysfunctional relationship, but you don't want to miss out on your true love, either. Someone who doesn't seem to be your match at first sight could be your soulmate; the opposite is also true.

Here is an analytic grid of possible results after the hug. It is only intended to guide the interpretation of your results, and nothing more, especially when you're dealing with people from cultures outside of North America:

1. **Butterflies in the stomach.** If the other person's body tenses up, and they don't know what to do next, they could be experiencing this. Don't be too swift in drawing this conclusion, though. Give them more time. **Unknown result until you decide to go the next step.**

2. **Wrinkling of the nose.** This signifies that your gesture disgusts the other person. Don't forget that even in this world full of nuances, clarity also exists. Apologize immediately and try to forget the humiliation. Leave. There will be others to meet. **Negative test.**

3. **Furrowed eyebrows and aggressive facial expression.** This shows that you are dealing with a potentially violent person. Move a safe distance away, then apologize…and leave. **Negative test.**

4. **The person is unnerved and gives you a slap in the face.** You have definitely crossed the line. Apologize and flee. **Negative test.**

5. **The person is surprised and says that it is too soon to get closer.** Bad timing. Apologize, respect the person's need for time and space, but do not assume that all is lost. **Could be a positive test.**

6. **The person is surprised but doesn't react.** You may be dealing with a person who takes too much medication, or a zombie. Check if they have a pulse and, preferably, leave. **More negative than neutral.**

7. **Wide-open eyes.** The person isn't surprised, thens miles or winks at you. This usually means that the person

is interested and paying attention. You've awakened the natural instinct of this person during physical contact. Hang around. **Positive test.**

8. **The person melts in your arms.** The connection with the person was such that engagement was evident and awaited. Eat the fruit of this natural connection with joy. **Positive test.**

9. **The person is surprised, but still melts in your arms.** The connection with the person was such that the engagement was desirable, but not anticipated. Do not ask questions. Go with the flow. **Positive test.**

10. **The person is surprised, but then kisses you with passion.** The synergy between you is real. Your prayers have been answered. **Great test.**

Natural attraction, infatuation, and sex drive is influenced by our DNA, which is encoded in our body. We can't ignore our body's call when searching for a soulmate because it's a vital part of the love equation. The sooner you find your "chemical" match, the better the next phase of discovery.

Lev's angle on the 4th chapter:

Is caveman test relevant in the dating?

Having graduated college with a major degree in Psychology (New Jersey, USA) and being in my late twenties, I can relate to the validity and observations of Andre's caveman test presented here. This test reminds me of the importance of non-verbal communication in our relationships, as well as the limits of such knowledge. It is a tool with many uses; we can learn how to present ourselves as confident leaders, potential mates, or even as adversaries pursuing a common goal. But, what are the weaknesses of such knowledge? Do these surface glimpses into an individual's internal worlds provoke more misunderstandings than they elucidate?

For starters, we are always subconsciously broadcasting messages. Our eyes, our face muscles, and even our posture reflect the nuance of thought beneath our surfaces. You have certainly noticed that when you yawn, your friend next to you is likely to do the same. By mirroring your actions, your friend conveys a similar state of mind. You are in agreement; your rapport is well- established and comfortable. However, this same phenomenon is not limited to yawns, however. We laugh when other people laugh, smile when other people smile, and though we understand the unspoken harmony between us, we rarely take notice as this exchange occurs. However, it is important to note that while you can identify emotions such as disgust, contempt, or attraction, you cannot determine the cause of this emotion.

Let's say you're having dinner with a lady at a beautiful Italian restaurant overlooking the bay. You mention a love of hockey, and she winces. What can we deduce from this? That she dislikes hockey? It's plausible, but there's also a possibility that in that particular moment, the chef opened the door to the kitchen and blew a stray piece of dust into her eyes. Perhaps she felt the warning rumbles of a painful migraine. Maybe the song that came over the speaker reminded her of the car accident she'd gotten into a few years prior, and the memory of her broken leg stung as she re crossed her legs. We are vessels of experiences, memories, and associations; therefore, we cannot predict anything beyond the most rudimentary of observations.

Ignorance isn't our only obstacle in discerning how our mates feel; we are biased creatures, susceptible to wishing upon lucky stars and blinding ourselves to all other wisdom. If we are of neurotic temperament, perhaps we might mistake shyness for discomfort, or reticence for disinterest. We then broadcast a barrage of anxiety tells in turn. Or maybe we will mistake a person's nervousness as an attraction to us and become emboldened. It is easy to set a trap for ourselves.

To this aim, I think Andre's caveman test provides a good starting place for discerning the relationship potential of one's mate. Be vigilant of body language, keep an eye out for impulsive tendencies, and don't be afraid to use your knowledge of non-verbal communication to send the right message. But, don't let your speculations tyrannize you. Go with the flow, be observant, and most importantly, have fun.

Tania's angle
on the 4th chapter:

A European woman's cultural view.

As a Portuguese lady from the late millennial generation, the cave-man test definitely has its worth. I would never think to run a test on someone with that specific intent, but on a subconscious level, I believe we are always responding to what we feel regarding proximity and physical contact to another person.

We have all somehow felt repulsed one time or another when touching another person. And I don't mean because they don't take a bath or something like that. I mean simply because in a way, we don't feel good with that person touching us, even with no particular reason.

On the other hand, we have all met someone we feel comfortable in close proximity with. This normally happens not only in romantic relationships, but with friends too. We Portuguese hug a lot. I greet most of my friends with big hugs (not all, but the closer ones).

The truth is: these kinds of tests are something that is always present in our daily lives whenever we meet someone. But traditionally, they go step by step: follow the eye contact, the physical language when speaking, the small touches… Well, I don't do them like a test; it's something that happens naturally, like recognition. It's a social ability that happens as part of my daily life. It's not that different from talking. It's just a part of socialization. On a dating site, you are going to meet someone with the explicit purpose of a romantic relation. My first contacts with a potential lover are normally when going out with friends, so having several encounters before any romantic step is given is never a waste of time.

Personally, it's a little strange to hug someone with the purpose of testing that person. These kinds of things flow naturally, sometimes with a bit of awkwardness. Like when I went to hug an old friend I hadn't seen in years, and he was completely stiff. Well, time changed the way we related (more for him than for me), but after that, I continued to respect his personal space.

In the seduction area, I see this almost like a dance, and a very nice dance that I wouldn't like to lose with a "first date exclusion test." Al-though, I do understand that for some people, the effort of several dates is not worth it. And if things develop to a date, we already have the "test dance" done.

So, there are different realities. There are different ways to do this test, but in the end, it's always there.

Claire's angle on the 4th chapter:

A young lady shares her experience.

As a Californian woman in my twenties, I have experienced those tests. Meeting someone for the first time after brief conversations over the internet can be daunting, especially when you both understand the only reason you're meeting is to see if you have sexual chemistry. Andre's Caveman or Cavewoman test is a fun way to get yourself out of your head and embrace the unknown. The test encourages you to focus on the other person instead of yourself and gage their physical reactions.

Humans communicate with their bodies more than they communicate with words. We send signals about our feelings out all the time. It's a valuable skill to be able to read a person this way, especially when you're trying to figure out if they like you or not. It's important to keep in mind that even though you can read someone's reactions, you can't be sure what they are reacting to. Not everything is about you, so stay out of your head. If you're really confused about someone's reaction, it's okay to ask them about it before giving up completely due to a 'negative test.' It's also important not to get caught up in whether or not someone likes you before you decide you like them. This is easily forgettable sometimes.

I commend André for prefacing his directions for the test by saying: "In order for it to work you need to have decent communication skills." That aspect is where we differ from Cavemen or Cavewomen; we respect the words or signals that are being sent and don't just take what we want. I appreciate that André introduces his test with caution and urges anyone who would try it to proceed only after they deem their subject mildly interested.

The point is to connect with that instinct; feel out the 'vibe' and go from there. If you're paying attention, you should be able to tell from across the room if a person is physically into you or not, and whether you're into them. Either way, confidence and respect are vital; unless the person is treating you horribly, nothing gives you the right to simply just turn around and walk away.

They're a person you're meeting; treat them well and with kindness. The website matched you for a reason. Maybe you don't have sexual chemistry, but you might be really good friend material. Again, I urge anyone who can't seem to read the signals being sent to simply ask; the dating process will be a lot easier if you're open and honest.

I think it's important to remember you will probably get a negative test if you run around hugging strangers. The people you're practicing this test on are individuals you've already spoken to on a dating site, and you have a bit of a feel for them. People you know better are probably better test subjects than someone you simply set a meeting with. Making snap judgments based off a few reactions you don't know the reason behind is never a safe bet.

Listen to your body, as André advises; reject an interaction if it doesn't feel right. If you like them, you should continue to get to know them; if they still aren't reacting to you favorably, move on and try not to take every encounter too seriously. It's hard to get out of your head once you're stuck there. But remember: don't let the feelings of others dictate your life.

Michelle's angle
on the 4th chapter:

This test originates from my culture.

Being born in Africa (birth land for human civilization) and now passing my mid-thirties, I would like to mention that the caveman or cavewoman test goes far back to the Old Stone Age. Also known as the Old Rock Age, when our ancestors knew little or nothing about sex education. They only anticipated what a basic sex behavior was, and if it turned positive, good for them!

Back in the modern age, the caveman or cavewoman test is very easy, and the test goes a long way in determining how you will be treated by any person you come across during your soulmate search.

During a caveman/cavewoman test, you will want to use your instincts to determine whether or not the person mutually consents to what you're proposing.

More often than not, a man (when getting to know a woman) will initially shower her with pleasing words that she evidently wants to hear. When that phase is over, he proceeds to prove more to her in his actions, in the sense that she can interpret his actions intelligibly without him voicing them.

Knowing this, if he decides to take it a notch further, this test proves positive (because a woman can actually deduct that at this point, he is seeking more, and he wants more). If the woman consents to what he's proposing, then she would not mind for him to take it a notch further.

85

This is where the inner intuitive test comes in. I believe this because at this point, the man knows the woman enjoys what he is doing, they both anticipate more. At this point, he has gotten to know a part of her that she likes to hear, and he will try to do everything possible to keep it that way.

As regards to this test, here are the possible outcomes (based on intuitive feelings):

COMPATIBILITY - It is a no-brainer that these two individuals are compatible; they enjoy the company of each other, and they appear to desire similar things.

LIKENESS - Based on the above test, they appear to like each other. Not only is this fact based on intuitiveness, but it is also evident in their relationship and the bond they have subconsciously created for themselves.

MUTUAL CONNECTION - It's a different case if a man likes a woman, but he is not ready to take it to the next level (likely due to past situations). At some point, when he does like her, lets her know his intentions, and decides to take it to the next level, she is totally down. That means she is mutually consenting to his proposal, inevitably forming a connection between them. It's like she is whispering in his ears; "Yes, I like you already... what are you waiting for?!"

As regards to using virtual dating sites, a caveman/cavewoman test is not farfetched. To avoid unimagined or surprising twists in action, it is important to test the waters before comfortably diving in. Sometimes, you might not know exactly what it is you are diving into.

Good luck!

Elisabeth's angle
on the 4th Chapter:

Is this a test for the millennials?

I must confess that "the caveman or cavewoman test" as represented in chapter 4 is absolutely fascinating to me. As a transplanted young girl in my mid-20's living in Boston, I have struggled to read and understand my partner's body language. For some reason I seemed to miss so many cues, which left me feeling depressed. But thanks to Andre's sharing, I'm learning a lot.

As I read his "Analysis of the results" and also study the test-based samples as presented in Chapter 4, I discovered that in few minutes Andre had explained in full detail what it took me years of trial and error to learn as a young girl. I couldn't believe myself when I began to find more insight and gained more knowledge with respect to this matter.

So, my advice is, when you appear before your romantic partner, have a clear understanding of his body Language. This can help you avoid misunderstanding, and thereby help you understand your partner's state of mind and, ultimately, help you communicate your own feelings and ideas.

As you read the description and suggestions in this chapter 4, try to picture the interactions you have had with your partner. So, carefully think about the role these discussions and suggestions play in your relationship, then carefully consider how you might use this information to enhance your relationship.

Best of luck.

Clara's angle
on the 4th chapter:

The shameless instincts of cavewomen.

I'm currently in my mid-twenties, living in Africa. As females, our cavewomen instincts are very active, similar to those of a man. We may not have the physical or otherwise obvious way to show when we are highly attracted to the opposite sex (like how men get physical reactions), but we do have body language, and other things going on in our minds and bodies that the other party can't see.

But before we go into that, let's find out what this caveman/cave-woman business is all about.

When people hear caveman/cavewoman instincts, the first thing they think about is violence. That is a common misconception. I promise not to lecture you. I simply want to demystify this subject.

The caveman/cavewoman instincts are biologically built in, meaning they are a part of us since birth. These things are not taught to us, such as our need to survive, to adapt to our environments, to feed, feel sexual love, clan or tribal loyalty and so on and so forth. Now that we have that out of the way, let's move to the sexual instincts.

I can't stop laughing at myself, because all I can think of is Marvin Gaye's song "Sexual Healing" especially the part that goes:

And when I get that feeling
I want sexual healing
Sexual healing, oh baby
Makes me feel so fine
Helps to relieve my mind
Sexual healing baby, is good for me
Sexual healing is something that's good for me.

Whew! I'm sorry. I just had to get that off my mind. Like Andre, I love music (especially the oldies). Okay, back to our cavewoman instincts. Yes, our bodies and minds do scream when we find a man attractive, and we start to strip the man naked in our minds. I have no intention to be vulgar, but it's important to know this part of us exists and it's not a bad thing.

88

No matter the culture, the tribe, religion, nationality or race, we all have sexual instincts (an exception includes asexuality). The good news is: the cavewoman in us is also wise, especially in choosing a soulmate. So even when the fireworks are going off in our heads, our cavewoman instincts kick in and tell us to slow down.

In the past, choosing a soulmate wisely was important, and women looked for men who carried particular attributes: a protector for times of war, a good hunter, a good farmer, a good investor (or simply wealthy), a care giver, sexual prowess, etc. As women, we still look for the same thing, but in a more modern way.

Now, physical attraction in the opposite sex varies in different women. So, we have different interests in men. Some are interested in the voice of a man and the manner in which he speaks, some women get attracted to facial looks or body structure, some are attracted to a man's composure, some women to his dress sense, etc.

How would you know when a man is also attracted to you? Here's my take on it:

Now ladies, this also varies in men. All you have to do is watch their body language. The following are most of the common clues, and are similar in men and women:

Eye Contact - Our eyes communicate a lot. They can convey our feelings, but they also have to convey the right message. If you stare him down, this sends a message that he has no effect on you, and that won't work. But, when you look at him and he looks back at you, look away, then slowly bring your eyes back to his. If he looks back, but with a particular tenderness, then Stage 1 was successful. But if he looks away with a straight face, he isn't interested.

Smile - It's important to give him a warm smile, as this makes the other party comfortable. So, give a wide smile by flashing your teeth in an admirable way. If he gives you a stiff smile, he is not interested. But, if he also flashes his teeth and his forehead stretches, stage 2 is complete.

Relax - When you relax, it shows you are comfortable. This makes the opposite sex comfortable, which helps communication flow. So, a way to show this is by leaning while you talk. This shows you want to be closer, but if you lean back it, it means you don't want to be with him. If he stiffens, he is not interested; but if he leans in too, stage 3 is complete.

Reaction to compliments - Compliment him if he looks good, or if you like what he is putting on. It's important to flatter him. Most men put in time to look good when meeting someone they like, so it's important to let them know you recognize the efforts.

Dress well - This goes both ways. Putting efforts into your looks shows that you like him. But when you don't, it sends the message that you don't care.

Physical contact - This is crucial. Men like to touch and to be touched. Some may not want to seem forward or like a creep, so they may try to keep to themselves. But, this is actually one way to sense or feel the sexual tension between the two of you. When talking, you could brush your fingers against the back of his hands, or you could place your hands lightly on his hands. If he continues talking without noticing, or removes his hand, he is not into you. But, if he looks down at your hand and smiles, or smiles and tries to keep the other hand busy, he's into you.

Pay attention to how he listens - It's good to talk about yourself. Letting a man into your world without him forcing it out of you makes him comfortable. But, it's also important to pay attention and to listen when he is talking or reacting to you.

Good luck!

Greta's angle
on 4th chapter:

The importance of non-verbal communication.

As a genuine mid-millennial woman from Tuscany, Italy, involved in a long-lasting relationship, I must confess that my chances to try the cavewoman test are long gone... at least with other men. I didn't meet my current partner through online dating, but in a similar way: There was no matching software involved, but our first encounter was a blind date.

Due to my marital status and how I got to know my companion, I think I can offer a different perspective: how do our baser instincts evolve throughout a decennial, monogamous relationship? How do we deal with non-verbal signals? Do we get to recognize them instantly in our partner?

As important as finding our "chemical" match is, learning how to keep that chemistry alive by understanding your other half's needs is vital. In my experience, unlocking non-verbal signals (especially the ones related to a mutual romantic and sexual interest) is part of the fun.

The sweetest memories of the first dates with my partner are related to a shy hug, a stolen kiss, or an unexpected touch. The tension created by the uncertainty ('does he feel what I feel? will this relationship work?') was paradoxically exciting.

I was thrilled to gather those non-verbal signals and interpret them. It is easy to assume that when the mystery is gone, the process will become less exciting. But in truth, I would say it is not. Of course, it is different, but not boring at all: It is actually hard work!

Although the caveman test is not designed for a long -lasting relationship that already exists (the three prerequisites are all way too present), we shouldn't take for granted. We know so much about our partner that we can cease reading the signs. For this reason, I think that not only anyone meeting a potential partner through online dating, but also long-dated couples who may or may not experience a downfall, could benefit from the test described by André. Or, any similar approach towards understanding non-verbal communication.

In a world filled with words, images, and information, we tend to forget about our nature and our instincts. Online dating sites might present a rational way of finding true love: one based on a matching model. But real life is full of nuances, and chemistry is a part of the game which cannot be predicted by an algorithm. Quite similarly, people involved in a long-dated relationship might tend to give importance to other things, such as children or work, and think it would be impossible to get back to that sort of innocence when the partner was still full of mystery and magic.

In my opinion, giving importance to non-verbal communication (especially when it comes to sex drive) could really make the difference for both new partners and long-dated ones.

Vanessa's angle on the 4th chapter:

Literal terms for getting physical.

I am a British lady from Lancaster, Great Britain, that has some experience in this area. I urge you to believe me on this one case. Why? Because I have been around for about twenty-six years (like I'm so old, right?).

I will take you through this gradually. I need you to imagine the Wolverine character in a state of calmness. I know you see all his huge and cute attributes. Now let me take you further to envisioning his angry state, where he unleashes the "wolverine with terrible claws" that Marvel wanted you to see (in case the name did not strike a chord).

Most of us have that Wolverine character hidden somewhere, waiting for the right time to unleash. This will help our illustration of the "Caveman and Cavewoman" instincts.

When a man is physically attracted to a lady or vice versa, you don't just walk up to the person and say "Booga! Booga!!" (like the caveman cartoon character). I like you so much... Come with me." I am sure this kind of approach would give you a restructured skull from broken bottles.

The word "Caveman and Cavewoman" can be misleading, so I had to clear that out. But the approach is quite different in both worlds. We will start with the Caveman approach. Since men are moved by what they see, when they sight an attractive woman, they try as much as possible to impress them. When they observe that they have gotten the attention of the lady, they start to emit the rays of attraction and watch out for body language. This is a response to their charm, and it helps determine the next line of action. If all things go well, you will find the woman resisting, but accepting. We can be that complex, but eventually, the man would get what he wants in the end (which is usually sexual gratification).

For the Cavewoman, I will not hesitate to mention that women are naturally stimulated by what they hear, so they use the "woman power" (which involves using her body) to communicate her intentions. The man speaks the word she wants to hear spontaneously, which speeds the process up. But this can only play out if the man totally understands the tune the woman wants him to dance to. Moreover, in a situation where the man is unable to paint the picture in front of him, the woman will take the bull by the horn and oversee the sexual initiation, if she chooses to go ahead.

Personally, my view in all this as a woman is that this approach started a long time ago, and I love it, because you talk less, but you get so much more from a man you are interested in. No doubt, the approach has its good and bad side, especially in cases when you are enduring your date and this kind of situation arises. Whatever the case, it is important to note that once you decide to go "Cavewoman test" you have to go all in, no matter the result. But choose your men carefully. Hence, my advice is to be sure about it and let it go "a step at a time," observing the opposite sex carefully. You will get to the top of the highest building using only the staircase. Ladies, trust your "Cavewoman" senses, and nothing else.

Yael's angle on the 4th chapter:

We call it "Tachles"

As a 26-year-old woman from Tel Aviv, I can see with all my learned wisdom why Andre reveals the eternal truth: we want to be loved. A simple hug is the essence of it, isn't it? The warm fuzzy feeling of warm hands holding you tight, capturing you with intent, making you feel there's no place safer than this relaxing and comforting moment.

However, for Israelis, tests are a vicious, untrue act. They're what we call: not "Tachles."

Tachles is like saying, "giving it to me straight" — and Israelis are very honest, straightforward creatures. Don't confound our inner souls with all publicized Israel politics. We are not fond of being tested, and we don't want to test anyone either. We will say things as they are, without sugar-coating it. This rule of thumb follows us in business, family, friends and of course, love.

Let me demonstrate:

I studied international law with a lot of people from all over the world, and dating was a part of that too. As a result, I dated this British guy. We decided to meet up on a date. But a day before our date, he calls and says, "Something came up, and I might not be able to make it." I didn't understand what 'might' meant. Would you, or would you not? Then I replied, "Ok. Does 'might' mean you can't make it?" Then he replied, "I might not." All I could think of is, "What's this 'might' all about? Can you or can you not?" After pushing harder at him to provide a definite, clear answer, he says, "No, I can't."

Needless to say, I didn't reschedule. All I thought about is, "Why couldn't he just be 'Tachles' to me?" I can only imagine how hard it is to date someone over and over again, just for the sake of being polite.

Andre's caveman/cavewoman test makes sense. As we're creatures of love, it's in our DNA to crave the sense of touch. Hey – don't get me wrong – I'm a hugger! However, I wouldn't want to be tested on, or to either test someone, if true feelings are not the motivator.

For me, the three prerequisites are crucial for the caveman/ cave-woman test, and I would add the following:

You must truly and deeply feel you want to hug the person in front of you, so deeply you would do it unconsciously.

Am I too overdoing? Or even naïve? I might be. As for me, honesty is sacred in love. One cannot exist without the other, and we build it, step by step, from the very first moment. I would want you to be "Tachles" with me, all day long and all night long, every single moment, for the rest of our lives.

Megan's angle on the 4th chapter:

Simplicity of the Caveman Test

A little about me first: I am twenty-four, and in my second year of a microbiology Ph.D. program. I am situated in Seattle, Washington.

I must say that the caveman or cavewomen test, regardless of a gender is much appealing. It relies on a set of logical rules based on human emotions and reactions. In this age of online dating, it is sometimes easy to forget the nuances of in-person dating. This test is a good reminder of what to keep in mind as one navigates the dating world.

From my own experiences I can tell you that physical advances from a man I am interested in versus a man I am averse to lead to very different bodily responses. As this caveman test suggests, it is very important to be aware of your partner's body language as you make your move.

An important takeaway from this test is that people broadcast much of their internal dialogue through body language. In fact, I would even go as far to say that one should not even attempt the caveman test if their partner is already displaying some of the negative reactions. While some men might say, "Take the chance! What is the worst that could happen?" to them I would respond, "Why waste everyone's time if you already know what the answer is?" However, if your partner has not been showing any positive or negative signs prior to the test, then I think this is a great way to test the waters.

As someone who does not like (nor have the time for) guessing games, I think it is also important to talk to your date about why their reaction was negative (if it was). Maybe she is not feeling well, or maybe you accidentally hurt her in some way, or maybe she just isn't as attracted to you as you are to her. Obviously, if the reason was one of the first two I listed, you should not take her reaction personally. There is still a chance she could be interested in you. However, if you never ask, then you will never know.

In conclusion, I like the simplicity of the caveman test. It builds on basic human biology and allows people to quickly gauge how their date is feeling. I think this test could be useful for both men and women, especially now that so much of dating is done online. But, as I eluded to in my paragraph above, body language can sometimes be deceiving. Use the test, but don't be afraid to talk to your date about the results!

Misunderstandings never lead to good results.

Interlude 1

As a rule, I try not to grocery shop when I'm hungry. When I do, I buy things I don't need, and invariably I overeat. It's hardly a problem unique to me. It's just human nature. I think it works that way with online dating, too. Here you are looking for a relationship—hungry for love, if you will—and suddenly, at your fingertips, are so many delicious-looking headshots and all those delicately baked profiles. The sheer abundance of choices triggers one of our most primal needs. It's little wonder, then, that in response we overeat. It was certainly that way for me.

When I decided to venture into online dating, the last thing I expected was that I'd become preoccupied with it. But that's what happened, and my newly minted obsession began as soon as I made the commitment to go online.

Before finally publishing my profile, I had invested an inordinate amount of time in writing what is really an idealized advertisement calculated to attract potential partners, and in choosing a fitting photo as my visual lure. I did not fabricate any of the details of my life, nor did I indulge in the subterfuge of passing off as current a flattering photo from the distant days of my youth, but I did spend countless hours packaging the goods. And once I went live, publishing my profile online, I found myself spending equally long periods searching out potential mates.

There were endless choices. Yet, having so many choices made any single decision all the more difficult to make, and I soon began second-guessing every choice I made. The very nature of the process had created false expectations and supported a growing illusion, crafted entirely in my mind, that I could have whatever I thought I wanted. It was thoroughly addicting.

In the past, people approached each other at bars, or asked a co-worker out during lunch. Meeting people in person allowed our intuitive sense to work quicker and more accurately. We had time to assess whether we wanted to dive deeper because our knowledge of people came from friends, co-workers and family, as well as direct contact.

But the choices were so limited in those days!

With online dating, I was getting the chance to meet the person of my dreams from the comfort of my home. When I received an email or a "like," I got a tiny surge of satisfaction. The best part was I could converse with a possible date, see if she was my type, and say adios at any time if things didn't work out. What's not to like? It's a lot easier to "peace out" when you're not looking someone in the eye or hearing the disappointment in someone's voice.

The trouble was I kept asking myself, "What about all the women I haven't met?" and "Is this as good as it gets?" I know it's a bad idea to compare people to food, but it was kind of like wishing I'd left room for the main course after eating too many appetizers. That's when it hit me, about two weeks in, that I was breaking my own rule. I was hungry for love, ravenous even, and here I was spending my day grocery shopping online.

My moment of clarity unfortunately didn't last. Women were beginning to respond to my online profile. They were making contact, and communication lines were opening. I was sure I was on the cusp of a breakthrough; that yes, indeed, online dating might well prove to be the path to relationship bliss.

I was, of course, completely delusional, my obsession now full-blown.

For both male and female daters, the shopping mentality is uniquely efficient online. In what other way would you make your way down aisles overstocked with different brands of the same thing? But the shopping approach does not translate well into face-to-face interactions, especially when separated by an exchange of emails and instant messages that too often serve only to make matters worse.

Don't get me wrong. Communication between people who may potentially date is a good thing. But, as I was about to learn, too much may skew expectations. As you'll soon see for yourself, I fell into the trap of reading way too much into the virtual communications I received. I didn't know the people I would soon be emailing and texting, and they didn't know me. Because of that, the words we exchanged would be affectless, devoid of the true emotion and nuance that can only be gleaned from real, face-to-face interaction. Yet, based on words alone I began to think I actually knew the parties on the other end.

It was the height of folly. It should never have happened, you may say. But remember: nature abhors a vacuum, and to fill that vacuum I did what so many of us do. I fashioned romanticized personas in my mind, idealized mental sketches of the partners I desired. To help flesh out those personas, I looked at the words and phrases contained in emails and texts received from women in whom I had an interest and gave them meanings that were consistent not with the reality of those women, which I couldn't possibly know at the time, but with the fictional personas I had crafted in my head. Call it confirmation bias of the virtual kind—the tendency to interpret new evidence as confirmation of one's existing beliefs or theories.

It sounds slightly crazy, but it's not—not even a little bit. Once again, it's just human nature. And, like countless others so ill-prepared for the world of virtual dating, I ran blindly through a doorway I now know was clearly marked "The Twilight Zone," and I plunged straight down the rabbit hole.

So... get ready for Part 2, in which I explore the transition from online to reality.

www.ingramcontent.com/pod-product-compliance
Lightning Source LLC
Chambersburg PA
CBHW071238020426
42333CB00015B/1528